Turn Right
At The Spotted Dog

Other books by Jilly Cooper
published by Methuen

Jolly Super
Jolly Super Too
Jolly Superlative
Superjilly
Supercooper
Jolly Marsupial
Class
Intelligent and Loyal
Super Men and Super Women
Work and Wedlock
The Common Years
How to Survive Christmas

Turn Right At The Spotted Dog

AND OTHER DIVERSIONS

Jilly Cooper

GUILD PUBLISHING LONDON

This edition published 1987 by
Book Club Associates
by arrangement with Methuen
First published in Great Britain in 1987

Made and printed in Great Britain
by Richard Clay Ltd, Bungay, Suffolk

To Hamish Aird with love
and extreme gratitude

Contents

Preface

This is the first volume of collected pieces to appear for five years. It is also the first volume to appear consisting entirely of articles which first saw the light of day in the *Mail on Sunday* as opposed to the *Sunday Times*, my previous platform. The move to the *Mail* more or less coincided with our move six months later to Gloucestershire from London. This will become clear to the reader, who will no doubt notice a more rural atmosphere among the choice of subjects. I am particularly pleased to see this book appear as it has given me the chance, once again, to repair the ravages of newspaper sub-editors and in some cases to add or expand a little bit where the exigencies of space led to hasty and sometimes ill considered cuts being made. In the piece about Princess Michael (which caused so much trouble), for example, I wrote 'Occasionally she can be manipulative' which the paper changed to 'She can be very manipulative'. This, I am sure the reader will agree, puts a different perspective on the matter.

Moving to the country was indeed a culture shock, not just to me but the whole family. There are lots of things about London, and dear Putney, that I miss. However, as I am sure will be apparent, there is no lack of material here to write about. Anyone who regards the countryside, and particularly that of our part of the Cotswolds, as a sleepy backwater will certainly have their eyes opened; the place is buzzing with incident, intrigue, gossip and humour – fertile ground indeed.

I would like to thank Stewart Steven, the Editor of the *Mail on Sunday* for allowing me to reprint these pieces. I am eternally grateful to him and his colleagues for constant guidance and encouragement. The fact that I found it necessary to make a point about restoring some of my original material was in no way a criticism. I always write over length, and newspapers have to cut somewhere. It is just the way they work. I would like to thank Annalise Kay for typing and invariably re-typing the manuscripts. I hope the reader will enjoy, as I did, looking back on the last momentous five years.

Bisley, Gloucestershire
June 1987

ONE

The Golden Middle

Everywhere newspapers are banging on about the good life beginning at forty. Sex appeal, we are told, has nothing to do with age. All the most admired women – Sophia Loren, Raquel Welch, Joan Collins, the Lindas Grey and Evans – are middle-aged. No one breathes a word about the traumas of the menopause any more.

And this week Princess Michael has jumped on to the bandwagon. Sailing through the pain barrier of being forty, she maintains she is entering a golden age of confidence and maturity, when she will trust her own instincts instead of listening to other people.

I wish I felt like that. At forty-seven, I should be in my prime. But I find myself increasingly riddled with self-doubt and about as buoyant at the moment as a snowball in a microwave. If I am honest, what really worries me about advancing age is how much longer I will go on attracting the opposite sex. I have an adorable husband, whom I love dearly. But he's in London half the week, and I worry, if I go off dramatically, that he'll go off me, and go off.

I don't actually want scores of men after me. I'm not talking about making out. I suspect having just emerged from seven months in enforced isolation finishing a book, I am missing all those consoling flirtations of everyday life that so boost the morale: the eye-meet in the tube, the chat-up at the party, the Gosh you're looking great, the wolf whistle from the man on the scaffolding, who can't see that the glow in your cheeks is a grid of red veins.

Perhaps I'm insecure because my sexual confidence took a bashing recently. Last year I did a television series, with a

13

wildly handsome actor. As the weeks went by, he gently chatted me up, and I found myself looking forward to each programme with gently increasing excitement.

Then on the final night, just as we were going on, he led me away from the rest of the panel. Did I mind, if he asked me something, he'd been screwing himself up to do so for weeks.

'Go on,' I said faintly.

'I'm madly in love,' he blushed furiously.

'Go on.'

'With the girl who does your make-up. Would you put in a good word for me?'

Talk about a woman of subsidence.

Then because of the book I only went to two parties this Christmas. On New Year's Eve at midnight, I found myself alone in the hall under the mistletoe with the handsomest man in Gloucestershire – and he merely pecked me on the cheek.

At the second party, a man who was into Chinese birth signs asked me the year I was born. Bravely in front of the throng, I told him. But instead of going into flattering paroxisms of disbelief, he said: 'You're a buffalo. Stolid, dependable, and totally humourless. Absolutely you, in fact.'

Buffalo Jill – hardly attractive, is it?

Another problem is that Joan Collins has raised all our middle-aged expectations. If Alexis can still inflame men in her fifties, why can't we? The trouble is that my generation were all warned at school that any wicked actions would show in our faces after a certain age, that if we wanted to look young, we should soft-pedal our make-up, wear pastel shades, and eschew smoking and drinking. And there's Alexis, the archetypal Mrs Wrong, breaking all the rules, behaving appallingly, lurid in fuchsia pink, chewing on cigars and permanently plastered with slap and on dry Martinis.

But to return to Princess Michael and her new confidence, I suspect she is batting from a position of strength because she is a dazzlingly beautiful woman with an attractive, adoring husband. The real pain barrier, because of the chronic shortage of spare men, must be entering middle-age if you're single, divorced or unhappily married and searching for a mate.

There's only one remotely attractive single man in his mid-forties in our part of Gloucestershire, and his feet haven't

14

touched the ground for five years. To find a man, you've got to turn into Mrs Wrong, and poach a husband. Perhaps that's what's making us married women so twitchy.

Princess Michael also has very young children, who give her the air and the illusion that she is a young mother. Young children, too, tend to think their mothers are perfect. Only when they become teenagers does scepticism creep in.

In the old days, for example, I never worried about clothes. But my children at sixteen and thirteen have now reached the beady, ultra-fashionable stage, when a collar too long, a trouser leg too wide, a skirt a fraction the wrong side of mid-calf – or mid-cellulite in my case – is beyond the pale.

Nor does it help that they go into paroxisms of mirth as they rifle my wardrobe.

'I had great success in that jump suit in the seventies,' I mutter sulkily.

'Pick-your-nose collars and disgusting flairs. Yuk!' they screech. 'You couldn't have got anyone in that, it's gross.'

And in middle age who am I trying to impress? Sucking up to the children, I wander round, shirt collars up, shirt tails hanging out from under my jersey – only to be told by my husband for God's sake to tuck them in.

Nor do I have the courage of my convictions any more. Learning that vamps were in fashion, I dug my old plunging black out of mothballs to address the Farmers Union in November, then getting cold feet rather than cold cleavage, rammed my feather boa into the plunge all evening. I was a bit nervous, too, as a middle-aged buffalo, that the farmers might pack me off to market.

Mid-January, of course, is the worst time of year for wrinklies. How glamorous all the mothers looked as they gathered in their fur coats for the end of term carol service at my daughter's school in December. Four weeks later, post Xmas, post school hols, battered by rows about impossibly untidy bedrooms, unwritten thank-you letters, and washing not brought down, the same mothers were virtually unrecognisable. Boots in Volvos, we all converged on the school like Valkyries, eyes tiny with tiredness, waists thickened by turkey leftovers and despair. My jeans are so tight at the moment, my eyes pop out every time I bend down.

15

One has to recognise, too, the signs of decay. At forty I wasn't bad. I could at least *count* my grey hairs. Now I'm pushed to find a blond one. My body skin looks OK but goes into tiny pleats when squeezed, which is admittedly not a lot these days.

Perhaps it's the Gloucestershire damp, but getting up in the morning, I find myself stumping into the bathroom as stiffly as the tin man in the Wizard of Oz. And if I don't get to an oculist and a dentist soon, I'll fail my MOT – never mind about jumpstarting my husband.

Nor, being such a drip about pain, am I likely to rush to health clubs and get my cellulite pummelled till I howl for mercy. I'd rather have my spirits lifted than my face. I tried lifting my face the other day in the mirror. But I just looked Chinese. Mrs Wrong may pull them in – but I can't see the local bloods queuing up for Mrs Wong.

Finally, even if I wanted to, it's not easy for the wrinkly to break out. Both the insecurity and the security are too great. No one is quicker on the draw than a teenager, which rules out any illicit incoming telephone calls. Last summer, to prove it, I actually had a date. My husband was in London. A friend was away and, with her blessing, her delectable husband asked me out to dinner. But, even with it all above board, I was so nervous I couldn't even put on my make-up. It'll come back, like riding a bicycle I kept telling myself.

The children hung around making helpful suggestions.

'You'd quadruple the men after you, if you cut your hair short,' yelled my son over the roar of the hair-dryer.

'Eyeliner goes on better if you pull your eyelids out,' said my daughter. 'And you're not wearing those gross patent leather sandals? Yuk!'

'Yuk off,' I snapped.

In fact I had a magical evening. But I did notice the moment we sat down to dinner, my date put on his glasses. I'd never seen him wear glasses before, and he's far too young to need them to read the menu. Alexis, and no doubt Princess Michael in her new confidence, would have construed it as a compliment that he wanted to see me better. I read it as distancing. In my youth, men whipped off their glasses when they wanted to fascinate.

As we got home at midnight, even before I opened the car

door, the front door opened, and there were my son, two dogs and four cats, brandishing magnifying glasses, looking for finger prints.

'How did you get on,' said my son.

Within minutes my daughter rang from a friend's house: How had I got on?

Next morning the same enquiry came in quick succession from my husband in London, my date's wife in Devon, my daily, my secretary and my very good friend the milkman.

'Well I didn't get off with him,' I admitted.

I suppose it was comforting that they were all so relieved.

Diamond Scullers Are a Girl's Best Friend

Henley was so wet this year it should have been rechristened Duckley. Happily I was accompanied by two young men so glamorous I hardly noticed the damp and cold. One of them was man-about-town, Johnnie Service. The other, a lynx-eyed naturalist called James McEwan, was just back from stalking leopard in Nepal.

'What a frightful season,' grumbled Johnnie, as we drove past battered banks of meadowsweet through the rain-dark tree tunnels leading into Henley. 'I've been pissed on at Ascot, Wimbledon, the Fourth of June and now Henley, and no doubt, I'll be pissed on at Goodwood.'

Despite the deluge, the band was whizzing through *The Marriage of Figaro* as we arrived and the carpark filling up with cheerful, broad-bottomed men in coloured jackets and pink and blue caps. Their mouths watered as they unpacked lavish picnics, and chopped up apple and cucumber to make Pimms.

One party had even laid out silver candlesticks on a snow-white table cloth. There's a Dunkirk (or rather a knife and forklands) spirit about the English which seems to make them enjoy outdoor jaunts even more if the weather is grisly.

Happily, too, Johnnie and James had perfect manners: so quick on the bottle and the umbrella that I never had a dry glass nor a raindrop falling on my head all day. Such a refreshing change from all those role-reversed males who snatch one's umbrella in a panic in case their perms kink in the rain.

In the distance, the river rippled olive green and shiny as a Harrods carrier bag.

'Shouldn't we be watching the races?' I asked.

'God no,' said James refilling my glass. 'Johnnie only

watched two races in four days last year.'

'Anyway it's considered frightfully unlucky to look at the water,' explained Johnnie.

All around us Bucks Fizz seemed to have been replaced by a foul concoction called Bellini, consisting of peach juice and champagne, and tasting like the remains of tinned fruit salad left too long in the fridge.

The rain was getting worse. A pretty girl in a straw hat and a blue mini squelched past in gum boots. Two Barbara Cartlands arrived in a large Bentley which progressed in a series of jerks, and ran over a deckchair to loud cheers. They were followed by a Range Rover full of yelling punks. One young blade had even dyed his rough-haired dachshund's beard flamingo pink to match his hair.

Johnnie looked disapproving.

'Do you know the difference between a Range Rover and a hedgehog?' he asked. 'The hedgehog has the pricks on the outside.'

James McEwan adjusted his panama hat, and said it was a shame the Henley colours were the same as the Argentinian national flag. Any minute now the band would break into 'I love Paras in the Springtime'. The Harrier Jump Jet set were also out in force, large ladies in larger hats swooping on one another with an antler clash of umbrellas: 'Deirdre, dar-ling, you're not still with Beardie?'

'My dear, I am,' screamed back Deirdre. 'Our house was so jolly cold last winter when the central heating collapsed, Beardie had to come back into my bed, and everything started up again.'

As the weather showed no signs of lifting, we went to lunch. Fortunately there was a bar halfway along the interminable queue so no one needed be without a drink for a second. A sweet girl in a boater told us about her ancient uncle who'd attended her sister's school play this summer.

'Uncle Willy's head kept lolling on to his shoulder, and we all thought he was nodding off. Only later we discovered he had this straw through his buttonhole attached to a hip-flask in his breast-pocket.'

Finally we reached the lunch tent.

'Good God, tinned potatoes,' said an outraged dowager.

'What is Henley coming to?'

After lunch we splashed round the stewards' enclosure in the drizzle. It seemed illogical that a Scotsman in a kilt was allowed in, but the *Mail on Sunday* photographer, who was much prettier, had to go into Henley to buy a skirt before she was admitted.

'Why does everyone look so ghastly?' complained a beauty, who appeared to be wearing nothing but gym shoes and a cricket sweater.

'Because they're all so common,' drawled her boy friend, 'Henley's even lower down in the social scale than Twickenham now.'

Certainly I was surprised, despite the sartorial restrictions, at how messy most of the women looked. As there's no definite skirt length this year, hemlines were all over the place; and those veiled pillboxes topped with ostrich feathers may have been stunning on the Princess of Wales, but on anyone else look like a parrot moulting over a meat-safe. Perhaps, too, because it's fashionable for women to crop their hair and wear men's suits and panama hats, only the men at Henley looked chic, whereas the women in their big hats and floating dresses looked over the top.

The prettiest woman was newscaster Jan Leeming, very suntanned in a white ankle-length Gini Fratini dress and white hat trimmed with pale pink roses. She was accompanied by that great rowing, whisky-drinking institution, John Snagge.

'It's so lovely, for a change,' said Miss Leeming, 'to have everyone clamouring to talk to John and taking no notice of me.'

I next had a quick whizz round Leander, the most famous rowing club in the world. They even have a president called Mr Rowe. In the bar, ancient members in pink caps, faded pink socks and moth-eaten boating jackets were radiating misogyny and reliving past triumphs.

I was reminded of a conversation overheard by a friend in the Travellers Club some years ago.

'Whatever happed to J.B.R.?' mumbled an old buffer from an armchair.

'Achieved the ultimate glory rowing for Oxford,' replied another armchair. 'Then spent the rest of his life in exhausted mediocrity.'

20

Last year, according to the club PRO, Mr Boswell, Leander had a fierce debate as to whether they should admit female members. Many debaters had seemed keen on the idea, and feelings were running high, when an old buffer struggled very slowly to his feet, and said: 'If yer put a cat flap in the back door, yer can be damned sure yer'll get all the neighbouring cats coming in as well,' and sat down again. He carried the day, and women were voted out by two to one. An unkinder touch is that even though women may now row in women's events at Henley, only male crews may compete in the Ladies Plate.

Anxious to banish any further suggestion of chauvinism, Mr Boswell changed the subject to the amatory prowess of the oarsman.

'He's the best lover in the world,' he said enthusiastically. 'With such powerful elbows he can keep going longer than anyone else.'

Not having a high opinion of rowers, I was sceptical of such claims, but as we came out of Leander, I was introduced to Christopher Baillieu, who is not only a silver medallist, but has also twice won the world championships and the Diamond Sculls. The Sebastian Coe of rowing, Mr Baillieu's beauty was even more gleaming than Miss Leeming's. I decided Diamond scullers were a girl's best friend after all.

Outside I found James and Johnnie extricating themselves from a comely but sulky-looking blond.

'She actually said she preferred community work to going to Henley,' said Johnnie in a shocked voice.

'Pretty though,' admitted James, 'for a girl at Lancaster University.'

The drizzle had turned to downpour again, opening up the coloured umbrellas along the bank like a vast herbaceous border. A balloon floated downstream to loud cheers.

'Well rowed, Eton,' went up the cry, as the Eton B team hissed by, their duck-egg blue oars flashing in and out of the pitted water.

Half a minute later, the Connecticut crew they'd beaten came by in floods of tears, and were clapped even more loudly because the crowd felt so sorry for them. It's all part of that kindness which also made the authorities fork out £425 last year for 'taking up and removing swans' from this stretch of the river, so they didn't get hurt or hurt anyone during the regatta.

Even one and three quarter hours getting out of the carpark didn't dampen our high spirits. Jolly gumbooting weather.

Sad-Olescence

Part One

In a month which saw the publication of a marvellous novel about a thirteen year-old, called *The Secret Diary of Adrian Mole*, it seems everyone is worrying about teenagers. Dr Miriam Don't Stoppard has been accused of urging adolescents on to sex rather than love, and the attention of the Press has been on teenage suicide and despair.

But the comforting thing I found – having talked over the last month to many thirteen year-old boys and their parents – is that our silly, woolly, flower-child generation seems almost by default to have produced a race of sensible, responsible, almost too-clear-eyed children.

The problem, for most parents today, is practising what you preach.

'We'd been to Ascot and carried on junketing,' said one father. 'It was rather incongruous to be woken at eight o'clock in the morning from one of the worst hangovers in recorded history to be told one's thirteen year-old son had been suspended from boarding school for sharing half a bottle of Sauterne with two friends.'

Many boys of thirteen, it seems, are allowed a glass of wine in moderation.

Alexander, whose father is a graphic designer, took me to lunch, ordered from the menu in perfect French, and sniffed the wine with great professionalism to see if it were all right.

'I don't mean to boast,' he said gravely, 'but I know a lot about wine. I never forget a bottle. For my younger brother Edward's birthday, we had Château Latour Bellevue 1971. I

23

must confess I did go overboard at our Royal Wedding party. I had three very strong Pimms, and I don't even remember Prince Charles and Lady Di coming down the aisle. But having once lapsed, I know I will be able to handle my drink in future.'

Single parents have the additional headache of trying to lay down a moral code for their children, which they intend to break themselves. Not only do thirteen-year-olds tend to dislike any display of sexuality (all the boys I talked to detested the thought of their mother in a ra-ra skirt) but also, as children of successive recessions, they are exceedingly beady about money.

One divorced woman friend said it was like having a Victorian father in the house. Having acquired a really delicious boy friend she celebrated by buying some Janet Reger underwear. Her son was outraged when he saw the bill.

'You really goofed there, Mum. Why spend a fortune on stuff no one's going to see?'

The cost of sex in fact seems to irritate children more than the moral aspect. Adrian Mole was incensed when his mother spent the family allowance 'which should by right be mine' on cigarettes and gin to drink with her boy friend. One mother I know, determined not to flaunt her new affairs, insisted on away fixtures. Her son was decidedly unamused.

'I was getting a new bike,' he grumbled, 'but now we can't afford it because my mother spends a bomb on baby-sitters every time she spends the night with her new man. Why can't they economise and sleep here?'

Most thirteen-year-olds, too, are perceptive enough to see through the most elaborate subterfuge.

'My father has a very nice new girl friend,' said one boy. 'But they are behaving in a very juvenile fashion. She pretends to be delicate and goes upstairs to lie down. My father then goes upstairs and pretends he's seeing how she is.'

Adrian Mole was not so generous. 'How can my father have carnal knowledge with that woman, she is as thin as a stick insect.'

At least if parents are separated, you don't get all the tensions of the young buck challenging the old stag for control of the forest. Rows in this instance can rock the house.

'The other night,' said one mother, 'my husband, Simon, was slightly the worse for wear when he changed the tropical fish

24

tank. Charlie, our son, was convinced Simon had squashed one of his eels.' The result was a great deal of eel-feeling. 'Charlie was upstairs leaving home, hurling dud batteries and the entrails of various disembodied radio cassettes into a case, shouting: "I'll never speak to Daddy again unless he apologises – and what's more you're on his side." Downstairs Simon was stuck into the Johnny Walker shouting that he'd never speak to Charlie again unless he apologised and what's more that I was on Charlie's side. I was tempted to call the international peace-keeping force.'

Richard, who's destined for King's School, Bruton, complained that his father had no sense of time. 'He's always sending me to bed early. I cannot stand answering the front door in daylight in my pyjamas.'

'My father tries very hard to be fair,' sighed one Radley boy. 'But I'm afraid it is quite beyond him. As he is the boss at work, he behaves like a boss at home, and is always ordering me to get him drinks and things. He once said "please" and "thank you", but his manners have deteriorated. I wish I could join a union.'

Today's child expects the family to be a democracy. One mother rather unwisely boxed her son's ears for taking a last chocolate biscuit. To this day he denies he did it. When she came home from work, she found her son and his younger brother had packed her two suitcases, put them outside the front door and double-locked her out, shouting through the letterbox they didn't want her to live with them any more. No entreaty could persuade them to open the door. She had to enlist the help of a girl friend to negotiate for over an hour before they let her back in again.

Despite claims that today's teenagers are permanently glued to the television, many I talked to were voracious and discriminating readers.

'I don't mean to boast again,' said Alexander the wine taster, 'but I am the fastest reader in the world. I've read the whole *Bible* except the Psalms, which I skipped because they lacked plot. I don't know what Freud would have made of Adam and Eve either. I was very moved on the other hand by the New Testament. Christ is a very credible character, but not St Paul, who changes far too quickly, like the Incredible Hulk, from being a complete weed to a man of huge stature.'

25

As a reaction to the woolly liberalism of their parents, boys of thirteen tend to be clear-cut in their attitudes. They disapprove passionately of smoking, pollution, and the nuclear bomb. On the other hand they were all tremendously involved in the Falklands crisis, and would have like to have joined the Task Force.

'I admire Mrs Thatcher,' said one, 'but I wouldn't like her as a mother. Whereas Shirley Williams would make a nice mother but not a good Prime Minister. Michael Foot looks too old for the job, but,' he added kindly, 'it might help if he used Grecian 2000.'

And that perhaps is the endearing quality of today's thirteen-year-old, his instinctive kindness.

'I loathe short-sleeved T-shirts,' said Timothy from Westminster, then seeing I was wearing one, added quickly: 'On men, I mean.'

'Please send me 50p,' wrote my son last term, 'but not £1, as I know you can't afford it.'

After a row, he'll be the first to make it up by bringing me a cup of tea, or after six o'clock a large drink. If I'm tired he'll make my bed or Hoover the house unprompted.

A thirteen-year-old boy from a very tough American school told me how his class had painted their form-master's chair-seat red. 'It was only when he came in next morning with the seat of his pants still covered with red paint that we realised it was his only suit. We felt so awful, we all clubbed together, and bought him a new suit for Christmas.'

The age of chivalry is alive again.

Part Two

Thirteen, aptly named unlucky, is a horrible age for a boy. Half child, half adult, he has to cope with all the confusion and indefinable longings aroused by puberty. Forgetting their own adolesence, his parents are often hurt and bewildered when he becomes moody and withdrawn, loving and co-operative one moment, fiercely resentful the next.

From a mother's point of view, however, there are compensations. Suddenly the scruffy boy, who had to be threatened to within an inch of his life to pick up a toothbrush, is cleaning his teeth three times a day, knocking back Listermint, having baths and washing his hair every morning. Soon envelopes, addressed to body-building equipment firms, start lying around in the hall. Dieting follows. The F-Plan must have encouraged more children to read than Enid Blyton.

A woman friend of mine also noticed a dramatic change in birthday lists. For his thirteenth birthday, she said, her son wanted computer games and remote-control aeroplanes. But for his fourteenth he's boldly indented for a sofa, a car, a double bed ('so I can roll over and get cool on hot nights') and a dinner jacket.

Buying clothes for them, of course, is a nightmare. Beau Brummel was not more exacting about the cut of his coat than a thirteen-year-old about the tightness and length of his trousers. Having witnessed the rejection of every slip-on shoe in the forty shoe shops in Putney, I also know how Prince Charming's footmen must have despaired of ever finding the glass slipper's owner.

And there's no getting away with handing a thirteen-year-old £25 and telling him to get on with it. He wants you there, to endorse his final choice.

Another revelation is the sexual sophistication of today's children. In a feeble attempt at sex education I took my son and some of his friends to the Natural History Museum. In the grandiosely named Hall of Human Biology I found scores of middle-aged parents barely suppressing their excitement as they pressed buttons which illuminated the sex organs of the body. I was dying to pick up a few tips myself but my son and his friends couldn't have been less interested.

'We did sex in Biology last term,' they said scathingly, and moved briskly on to the tarantulas in the next room.

Another woman friend was deeply embarrassed when her house was burgled recently. Her thirteen-year-old son didn't give a damn that the record player, the television and his tape deck had been stolen. He was outraged, as he kept telling the police, that three sex mags had been pinched from under his mattress.

Some parents worry that their sons will be corrupted by watching X-films on video machines in darkened rooms at ten o'clock in the morning. But one must remember that in boys a desire for titillation goes hand in hand with intense romanticism. There is also a huge gap between theory and practice. Anyone can read endless technical books telling them how to ride, but it doesn't mean that when presented for the first time with a large thoroughbred, bounding with oats, they will be able to stay on its back round the course at the Horse of the Year Show.

And despite their professed knowledge and sophistication thirteen-year-olds still get things deliciously wrong sometimes. 'Elizabeth', wrote one boy in his Common Entrance Scripture exam, 'was not able to have babies because she was a Baron.'

I asked two thirteen-year-olds about to go to all-boys public schools whether they felt they'd be missing out on contact with the opposite sex.

'Well there's no point in having girls at prep school,' said the first, 'because one doesn't really need them. But it would be nice at one's public school, although humiliating if one went to a school that allowed in only a few girls. There wouldn't be enough to go round.'

'At my school,' said the second, 'it's OK because you get O-level French girls. And when you're older they take you in a van to dances at girls' boarding schools, and you smoke and drink and go into the bushes.'

Denied girls their own age, thirteen year-olds tend to fall for much older girls.

'During the holidays,' said Timothy, an exceptionally beautiful boy in his second year at Westminster, 'I wrote to one of the 6th form girls, she's eighteen, telling her how much I admired her. She wrote me a very nice letter back, saying she looked forward to seeing me next term. But back at school I felt very shy so I cut her dead. I'm sure she was hurt – I was miserable.'

Sad-olecence . . . we plot, we dream and when the moment comes we funk it. Pin-ups for thirteen-year-olds tend to be women who are beautiful, gentle and maternal: Jan Leeming, Selina Scott, Lady Diana.

Although Alexander, who went to a London boys' school, said he wasn't turned on by Lady Diana. 'But you mustn't blame her,' he added quickly, 'because I haven't met anyone who turned me on yet.'

'None of my class have girl friends, except one boy who's got

28

a German pen-friend. He brings her letters to school and tries to read them out. No one's interested because they're in German.'

By contrast the thirteen-year-old boy at a comprehensive school seems sexually light years ahead. John, who is tall and very good looking, goes to Eliot Comprehensive in Wandsworth. According to his mother, girls ring him up all the time. Unlike the public school boy he only dates girls of his own age.   'I wouldn't dream of going out with a fifteen-year-old,' he said grandly. 'I don't need to resort to older women. But it's equally frowned on to cradle-snatch an eleven-year-old.'

He admitted contempt for public school boys.

'Because school fees have rocketed many parents run out of money and suddenly have to send their sons to Eliot. The sons are so wet they get ludicrously excited at the thought of girls and say: "You don't actually talk to them, do you?" They also refuse to admit that girls are as bright as boys. They're depressingly sexist.'

Despite timidity and sexist attitudes, however, the public school boy does have honourable intentions. One headmaster showed me a letter he had confiscated in a Latin class: 'My darling Virginia, I hope to see you soon because I really love you a lot. You are really beautiful, in eleven years will you marry me? Please return your answer quickly. Lots of love, Mark.'

Finally, I like the way even the hoariest old chestnut gets updated. One woman friend, in despair that her son was ever going to pass his Common Entrance exam to Marlborough and driven crackers by his refusal to work in the holidays, ordered him to write an essay on a day in the country. Ten minutes later he returned with the following:

'My day in Soho.

'I decided to spend my £15 birthday money on a trip to Soho. Suddenly my eyes fell on a beautiful woman, who was wearing a red dress and red lipstick. She handed me a card saying: "The name's Mabel, and I cost £12 plus VAT." I accepted her offer, and we went to her bedroom. Her brown hair looked lovely in the light, so we both stripped off and had a lovely time. Suddenly her digital alarm went, and she said: "Time's up."

'I got dressed. Mabel gave me a receipt and said, "See you next week". It was well worth the money.'

Trial By Jury

Being self-employed, I've always dreaded jury service even more than shingles. Alas, last month, my luck ran out, and I was summoned to do my stint at the Old Bailey.

Having just joined the *Mail on Sunday*, and also having two books to finish, I was thrown into complete panic. What would happen if I was put on a tax case that ran for ever like *The Mousetrap*, or even worse some Ripper trial so riveting that I'd get thrown into prison for not keeping my trap shut at dinner parties?

The most unkindest cut was that my dear dog-walking friend, Tristram, had also been summoned for jury service at the Old Bailey, but starting the week before me, so we couldn't even be new girls together. On the eve of his debut, we shambled gloomily round the common, discussing what we could wear on our respective first days to compel the counsel to chuck us out.

I opted for a pork-pie hat and at least a dozen National Front and CND badges.

'I'm going in drag,' countered Tristram sulkily. 'I'm jolly well wearing my party frock.'

Next day I took off to Normandy for a week to steady my nerves. At least if I acquired a sun tan, I might while away the boredom wowing a few barristers.

Wednesday

First jury day dawned. Rose at six to waddle the dogs – so fat from holiday gluttony I'd be lucky if I got into the jury box. The court had already informed me they'd pay my fares if I travelled by public transport. Just dickering between 22 bus, which takes at least two hours in the rush hour, and alternative one and a

30

half mile walk to station, followed by two tube changes, with half mile walk the other end, when my husband rang to say the Kings Road was blocked solid, so I'd better get a mini cab, and that he'd divorce me if I found anyone guilty.

As I left, the dogs looked at me in stunned disbelief. Having deserted them for a week, was I abandoning them again?

Just reached Old Bailey on time. Fought my way through blue forest of policemen to find a large crowd of first-day jurors, milling all forlorn, outside the Jury Bailiff's office. Most of the men were sweating in suits. The women, Thatcherized in blazers, shirts with pussy cat bows, and pleated skirts, looked at my jeans askance. Perhaps they should form a Metropolitan Pleats force.

The next half hour was spent with everyone asking everyone else if we'd come to the right place. Then a white-haired man in a black gown made it seem even more like the first day at school by taking a roll call, and we all trooped into court.

Suddenly, in the back row, I saw a terrific chum: Mr P who runs the local off-licence. With any luck we'd be twelve good men and Ben Trueman. Gave loud shriek to attract his attention and was sharply shushed by black-gowned lady. Mr P went pink and waved back discreetly.

We were given a pep talk about never discussing any case we were on with anyone but our fellow jurors, and not taking it to heart if we were challenged.

'It's nothing personal,' explained the black-gowned man kindly. 'Prosecution might just want more ladies to balance a case.'

'Mrs Higgins was on a drugs case last week,' said a fat woman behind me. 'Defence threw out anyone who was wearing a tie.'

Masterminding the Old Bailey must be rather like running a vast all-the-year-round Wimbledon, where you have to find twelve new umpires for each match. The staff was expected to produce different juries for the twenty-five courts on cases, which may be extended for days because of legal squabbling, suddenly terminated because of insufficient evidence, or unaccountably held up because the judge wants to play golf. As a result the hanging about is ludicrous.

Next all the first-day jurors were sent up to the vast jurors' canteen, where people were sitting round, chatting, reading, knitting and doing crosswords. A few dedicated individuals were trying to work: a lady in a caftan and sandals was indexing a biography, an architect had rather ostentatiously commandeered a whole table to draw plans of a house. I attempted to write but found it impossible to concentrate. Every so often the tannoy crackled incomprehensibly, or a black-gowned lady came in, reeled off a list of names and bore a group off on a case. It was like being trapped in some foreign airport, where you daren't get stuck in a book in case you don't hear your flight being called.

For the next ninety minutes, Mr P from the off-licence and I wrestled with the *Sun* crossword, and discussed the drinking habits of many Putney residents. At noon, my friend Tristram drifted in. He'd abondoned the idea of a party frock in favour of a pale grey suit. Having been *in situ* for a week, he was able to regale us with all the local gossip. In one corner huddled a butch lady with a crew cut, who, having been objected to on five successive cases, was thinking of consulting an analyst. Another man, said Tristram, had had a heart attack when he was challenged, and yesterday a Chinaman had been sent home for good because he rolled up with an interpreter.

'Some people 'ave been 'ere eight days, and 'aven't 'ad a case yet,' said a crone in Kit-e-Kat pink, scratching a midge-bite.

At 12.45, the black-gowned lady returned and told me, Mr P and twenty-two other first-day jurors to go to lunch, and to report to Court 13 at two o'clock sharp. Tristram, who'd been told he could go home for good, whisked me off to the pub to meet his fellow jurors, who included a lady gardener from Hackney parks, and a woman who cleans engines in the Woolwich Tunnel. I was amazed how depressed they were that their jury stint was over. Most of lunch was spent discussing whether their employers would notice if they didn't go back to work till Monday. Later they moved on to the judge on their cases. Every morning and afternoon, the clerk had evidently lined up fifteen toffees on the ledge in front of him, which his lordship had noisily sucked throughout the case.

They were all gleefully telling me about a fellow juror who'd gone all the way to Harrods in her lunch hour to buy a dress for Ascot, and been fined £60 by the judge for getting back eighty minutes late, when I suddenly glanced at Tristram's watch, and saw to my horror it was five past two.

Belting back to the Bailey, I couldn't remember the number of the court I was meant to report to. Finding a vaguely familiar group in the foyer, I followed them upstairs. It was only when an eager woman in a tweed skirt started spouting in front of an statue of Elizabeth Fry, and everyone began saying 'Right' and 'Oh my Gard', that I realised I'd joined a group of Nancy Reagan clones on a tour of the building. I was just having hysterics at the prospect of being fined £100, when I was gathered up by Mr P from the off-licence, saying our case on Court 13 had been adjourned, so it was back to the canteen.

The rest of the afternoon was spent being herded into lifts, hanging about outside various courts, and being herded back to the canteen again. Only thing missing was a commentary by Phil Drabble.

Finally sent home at 3.30. On endless bus journey, I listened to two women who'd just come off a skinhead mugging case.

'I knew they was guil-ee,' said the first. 'Then I see them looking at me, finking we'll do 'er in four or five years when we get art, so I said: "Not guil-ee".'

Thursday
Rose at six to walk dogs in already punishing heat. No time to wash hair. Having walked to Putney Bridge, I experienced commuting for the first time in thirteen and a half years. Did not enjoy it. Now know what bunched asparagus feels when it is plunged into boiling water. Most of journey was spent clamped against hotly sweating young man, clutching envelope on which was written: 'Nigel: too late to open. Please provide sperm whale figures for tomorrow's meeting.'

Second morning at Old Bailey was just as much of a shambles as the first. Institutionalised feeling heightened by hospital smell in ladies loo, where a magenta-faced blonde was cleaning her neck with a roller towel dipped in TCP.

Nearby a large woman (with a motif on her bag of a womble playing the banjo) was holding a justifiable indignation meeting because she was not being compensated for her jury service.

'If you're an 'ousewife, you get nuffink, cos you're not employed. Dottie gets ten pounds a day, cos she's a sekketry.'

33

Her friends all clicked their tongues sympathetically.

At 11.30, we were summoned to a court on the ground floor. On the way we passed a statue of Bloody Mary the first, brandishing an orb like a hand-grenade. Why that vicious old bitch, the incarnation of persecution and bigotry, is honoured in a court of law is beyond understanding – perhaps because she kept the legal profession constantly in work.

We then sat for half an hour outside the court admiring Charles II's excellent legs. Lawyers sauntered back and forth with the elitist swagger of airline pilots at Heathrow. Policemen bustled in and out. Evidently there was a technical hitch.

In our group was a railway engineer with Reagan black hair and a handsome foxy face who was totally demoralised because he'd already been objected to on three different cases.

At long last, we were summoned into court, and twelve names including mine, Mr P's and the railway engineer's were drawn out of a hat. We filed nervously into the jury box under the coldly appraising gaze of the two counsels. The defence barrister, who had heavy-lidded eyes like Charles II, threw out a lady who looked like Mary Whitehouse.

Suddenly I desperately wanted to be accepted and tried very hard to look like Richard Baker – respectable and compassionate at the same time. It worked – I was sworn in. So was Mr P and, to his amazed joy, the railway engineer. The rest of our jury included an ex-clippie, a transport manager, a pretty barmaid, a part-time secretary, a sweet German housewife, a gardener, a Belfast bricklayer, a forklift truck driver, and an unemployed swing attendant from Hackney parks who had a huge love-bite on her neck.

The railway engineer's cup really ranneth over when we selected him as our foreman.

'He's tall, and a foreman should be tall,' said the part-time secretary approvingly.

Indeed the railway engineer seemed to have gained two feet in the last five minutes.

At last we were going to do some jurying. But not a bit of it. Another hitch, and the judge dismissed us until after lunch.

'That judge lives in Putney,' said Mr P in disgust.

'Customer?' I asked.

'No, buys his wine at Peter Dominic.'

Cheered up by jolly lunch with my publisher. On my return, nice German housewife gave me a peppermint to conceal the Muscadet fumes, and the Belfast bricklayer gave me a tip for the 3.30 which I couldn't use – owing to broken telephone. Finally we started our case, which had a beautiful defendant, and was utterly fascinating, but which I can't tell you a thing about in case I go to prison.

Unable to face tube home, I took alternative bus route, and got hopelessly lost. Tramping the length of Park Lane, I was approached outside Hilton by a Dutchman who was convinced I was one of the singers in the Eurovision Song Contest.

Home by 7.30 with three blisters, and announced I was at last on a case.

'Did you wear a wig?' asked my daughter in awe. Replied that I soon would if I didn't get a chance to wash my hair.

Friday
Even hotter and more muggy. Limping to Putney Bridge, met fellow dog walker returning from Common with two Great Danes, green from rolling in deceased hedgehog. Before I could leap away both dogs greeted me ecstatically. Despite liberal spraying of Diorissimo, stench clung pervasively. Could always say I was upholding the forces of law and ordure.

Arrived at the Bailey to find the usual shambles, with fellow jurors banished from the court by new hitch. All the women, except nice German housewife, had reverted to trousers. A new intake of jurors had just arrived, giving us all a great feeling of superiority. Did we really look as bewildered and over-dressed on our first day?

To pass the time, I smiled winningly at the defence barrister, who was quite good looking, but who promptly averted his eyes like the maiden of bashful fifteen. Soothed my bruised ego with excuse that he must be terrified of sucking up to the jury. However when we returned to the canteen, a tea lady informed me that Gayle Hunnicut had been on jury service recently, and while she was in court, no one ever looked at the judge.

Midday:
By some miracle back in court. Noticed prosecution counsel's

35

nostrils flaring ominously. Had he caught a whiff of deceased hedgehog? A few minutes later, our case was adjourned for ten minutes. The barmaid and I looked at each other longingly, then nodded, and scuttled out to the nearest pub, hotly pursued by our foreman and the Belfast bricklayer. Returning after several doubles, the bricklayer gave me five to one we'd be adjourned till after lunch. Our foreman said he'd now conduct the entire jury in a chorus of 'Nellie Dean'. Yo, ho, ho and a bottle of Rumpold, I sang happily. Mercifully, as the bricklayer had predicted, the hitch had acquired new technicalities, and we were dismissed till after lunch.

Feeling guilty about my unseemly debauch, I refused to be persuaded back into the pub, and went up to the canteen for a frugal cheese salad.

After lunch, even though our case wasn't finished, we were taken upstairs and locked into our little jury room, which contained a large table, twelve chairs and copious net curtains – presumably to knot into an escape rope if they forgot to let you out. The foreman then said: 'Don't all talk at once', which we promptly all did. Why do I always believe the last person I haven't listened to?

2.40. Back in court, case naturally adjourned till Monday. Feel very strongly that when you are summoned for jury service, your family and employees should be warned that you will not automatically be closeted in court every day from ten till four. One juror dismissed at lunchtime earlier in the week had evidently caught his wife in bed with the lodger, while a stern female boss had rushed back to her office at a quarter to twelve to find the entire staff had played truant, except one typist who'd raided the drinks cupboard and was ringing America.

Made mental note to bang front door noisily and shout 'Cooee!' several times when I get home, to give senior cat time to straighten his fur and smuggle neighbouring tabby out on to roof.

Monday
After frantic weekend, was unable to face commuting (how the hell do people do it every day?) and ordered a mini cab. Desperately worried about senior dog, who was going into a decline at my continued absence. Contemplated changing her

name to True, then I could bring her into court as an essential accompaniment to twelve good men.

As usual my fellow jurors were kicking their heels outside court. By now we all knew every marbled varicose vein on Charles II's legs. The swing attendant had acquired another love-bite. The Belfast bricklayer arrived in a panic because he'd met a familiar-looking girl and carried her bag all the way from the tube before he realised she was the defendant on our case.

Back to the canteen, where to my amazed delight I found Donald our postman among the first-day jurors. A resplendent redhead, Donald is even more of a fund of Putney gossip than Mr P from the off-licence. Recently our entire street went into mourning when he was transferred up Putney Hill to another beat.

Donald the postman was just telling Mr P and me how he'd been bitten by a horse while delivering a parcel last week, when another friend, a literary lady from the British Council, rolled up. It was getting more like a cocktail party every minute.

'Meet Donald,' I cried. 'He's a distinguished man of letters.'

'Really?' she asked, looking very excited. 'What's he working on at the moment?'

'Mailbags,' I said airily.

It was as well, perhaps, that we were called back to court for the summing up by the two counsels. I found myself totally agreeing with Richard Ingrams that 'when lawyers talk about the law, the normal human being begins to think about something else'.

Fortunately, by contrast, the judge's summing up was blissfully succinct. As we went up in the lift, even Mr P had to admit he was a clever fellow. 'Even,' he added grudgingly, 'if he does shop at Peter Dominic's.'

The lady clerk locked us into our jury room: 'You may now resume your deliberations.'

'Didn't know we'd taken them off,' cackled the ex-clippie.

Happily we reached a unanimous verdict in five seconds flat, then let everyone finish their cigarettes so it appeared that we had thrashed the matter out.

As we came out of court, Donald the postman ambled past on his way to lunch, saying wasn't Charles II's spaniel exactly like Lady Weldon's at Number 8.

Tuesday

Suicidal about not being able to work, and because my husband, children, dogs and cats were getting increasingly ratty at my extended absence. Took another mini cab.

Found fellow jurors equally ratty. Were we going to endure more days of hanging about before we got on our next case? Our foreman and Mr P were frantic to get back to work. The barmaid had hayfever and was getting behind with her housework. The German lady was fretting about greenfly. The swing attendant had a necklace of amethyst love-bites. Everyone was praying we weren't put on a long case, when out came the Jury Bailiff.

'Nothing much on this week,' he said. 'You've done a good stint, so go upstairs, get paid and push off home.'

We all stared at him utterly aghast. Looking round I realised not only how fond we'd all got of each other, but also how insulated I'd been over the past week from the telephone and the doorbell, and the demands of family and friends. I felt quite incapable of facing the outside world. Dispiritedly, we had a last cup of coffee in the canteen, vowed to keep in touch, and at least meet for a Christmas drink every year, then collected our wages.

On reflection, however, when I consider I was only in court for about five hours in five days, and how much self-employed time was wasted with the excuse that it is one's duty as a citizen, I can't help feeling there are many unemployed people who would leap at the chance of serving on a jury and having something practical and remunerative to do.

We allowed ourselves to be shunted around because we became the depersonalised part of a system, about which many people, including Lord Denning, have grave doubts. Despite the unruffled good nature and consideration of the Old Bailey staff, I feel any contempt of court is aimed principally at the jury.

Nude Without Violin

Having left London in a heat wave, to spend the day on Brighton's nudist beach, I was slightly nonplussed to be greeted by sullen skies and icy winds. As I shivered fully clad on the damp shingle, ludicrously disguised in dark glasses with my hair in a pony tail, the only thing bare was the beach.

I was about to freeze to death when a faint gleam of sunshine appeared, and a gloomy man in maroon started shoving a metal detector over the pebbles. Next a handsome youth, clad from top to espadrilled toe in French navy, sat down beside me, and bravely undressed to his candy-striped underpants.

With the whole beach to choose from, why did the metal detector man feel the need to circle accusingly round and round my towel as though I was sitting over the *Masquerade* hare. French navy next door, having cautiously removed his underpants, hastily pulled them on again as the metal detector approached.

11 a.m.
Hurray – sunshine, and a vast couple, both looking nine months gone, crunched past us, whereupon she stripped down to her straw hat, and he to the altogether. Odd that he had spent so much time training his spare grey locks over his bald cranium when he was displaying so many acres of spare flesh elsewhere.

Predictably, the man in maroon was soon bearing down on them until, suddenly deflected by a winsome youth in dungarees, he absent-mindedly ran his metal detector over the fat woman's stomach. Both gave off noisy squawks – perhaps she was on the coil.

The temperature soared, I was down to my bikini, and the
39

beach was filling up, not only with nudists, but also with fully clad spectators, including a Chinaman in an Old Rugbean tie, and an Old English Sheepdog. Several young lads were even frolicking in the sea, which caused a man with a beard and rather too much jewellery to whip out his binoculars and display a keen interest in marine biology.

Nearby, a hefty new arrival bent over, grunting, to remove his socks, and, peering through his legs, caught me looking at him. The trouble with nudist beaches is that everyone hides behind books trying to pretend they're not looking at everyone else the whole time. Even Jeffrey Archer goes unread.

Noon
After erecting a Wrigley's spearmint parasol with much wiggling, the fatties were waddling down to the sea for a dip. I gingerly removed my bikini top, only to find an ancient couple had parked themselves on my left. The husband having removed everything except a flapping corn plaster was gazing goatily around him. His wife, rigid with disapproval, remained in her woollen cardigan and floral shirtwaister.

'It's disgusting, Gilbert,' she snapped, mouth shutting like a trap. 'If they could only see themselves.'

She was right of course. The large majority of people on the beach were men well over fifty, labouring under the illusion that it doesn't matter what shape you are as long as you're brown all over. Even worse, their ludicrous uniform is to wear nothing but dazzlingly blancoed gym shoes and a little peaked cap to hide the lack of hair and cast fascinating shadows over the eyes. Half of these ageing satyrs spent their time standing in one place, trying to look noble and boyish like Michelangelo's David. The rest never stopped sauntering round the beach as though they were modelling birthday suits for the very much fuller figure. Crunch crunch crunch went their white gym shoes on the pebbles.

I was so transfixed by a butch lady with a huge bust, a kind of Alice B. Topless, who was oiling her little husband with great slaps that echoed across the shingle, that I didn't notice in time that a bespectacled redhead had sat down on my right. Clearing his throat, he peeled speedily down to his freckles.

'This is the first time,' he said thickly, 'I have had occasion to

40

divest myself on a nudist beach. I am what is commonly known as nervous – goodness, these pebbles are sharp.'

Half an hour later, he had not drawn breath. The only pity, he said, was that the lads at the Water Board where he worked would never believe he'd divested himself. Perhaps I could be persuaded to take a photograph of him. Frantic to change the subject, I made the fatuous observation that he must have lots of pressure in his job. Any minute we'd be talking about stopcocks.

Bored with sunbathing – his white skin was already tinged with rose – he produced a camera, and began snapping all and sundry, to their intense irritation. He was just poised to capture goaty Gilbert leering at a buxom brunette, when Gilbert's shirtwaisted wife gallantly flung herself in front of the camera.

Suddenly my red-headed friend turned on me. 'You're the girl who writes for the *Mail on Sunday*.'

So much for my disguise as an undercovered agent.

'No I'm not,' I bleated. 'I'm always being mistaken for her, but she's much younger than me – and thinner.'

'Could have sworn she was you, what's her name?'

'Katharine Whitehorn,' I said firmly.

Mercifully he was distracted by a comely blonde undulating down to the sea with a chain-mail bottom from lying on the pebbles, and promptly snapped her for posteriority.

By afternoon, which was early closing day, the beach was enhanced by some really beautiful people of both sexes. The standard pick-up practice is for a boy to lob pebbles on to a girl's bare back. If she doesn't rise mentally or physically, he then goes and swims, and shakes his wet hair all over her. A flurry of Do you Minds invariably follows, and an acquaintance is struck up.

The most absurd female fashion was three naked girls parading round with those space antennae bobbles clipped on to their heads. As though the Martians had landed.

Just below me a plump man, wearing nothing but co-respondent shoes, was watching a blond youth in Bermuda shorts playing drakes and drakes. Soon he was joined by a friend. 'Have you seen Pedro recently? Raoul says he's all of a sag, isn't age cruel? Ooch!' he screeched, leaping in the air as he was goosed by a jolly Labrador.

Spectators were also out in force – mostly middle-aged men in suits. Behind me, a granny in a camel-hair skirt, her two daughters and their assorted yelling offspring had lined up their deckchairs for a jolly good gawp.

'Look at 'him,' cackled Granny. 'Tattooed all over, and I mean all over, must'ave hurt. Stop sucking that pebble, Natalie, you don't know where it's been.'

By four o'clock I was dying to swim but too nervous to run the gauntlet of all the eyes. Just as well, for suddenly a large gang of black youths rolled up in immaculate white suits, and stood on the brow of the beach, gazing down at the stretched-out bodies. In such a role-reversed situation, I felt we ought to rise up and do a tribal war dance to entertain them. Aware of incipient menace, male sunbathers started rolling over on their fronts, women huddled into the shingle.

Next minute, the black gang came whooping and zigzagging down the beach, leaping over bodies, ripping away towels.

'Did you ever see such a grotesque sight, man?' howled the leader, slithering to a halt behind Alice B. Topless. Instantly they formed a barracking chanting ring round her.

'Do something, Hildred,' hissed Alice, quivering with rage. Little Hildred very sensibly cowered behind Iris Murdoch, until the gang got bored and bounded off down the beach to mob-up one of the satyrs, who was nervously employing a C & A carrier bag as a fig leaf. Finally, with a yell of 'Effing fairies', the gang took off towards the West Pier, and we all heaved a sigh of relief.

Unable to bear the heat any longer, I crept down to bathe. Those pebbles were such agony to walk on, it's impossible not to wobble. Entering the sea, I was startled to see two red bums sticking up in the air. They turned out to be two youths diving for pebbles. I suppose boys will be buoys.

Just as I was up to my waist in blissfully cool green water, I realised I'd left my watch on, and had to stagger back up the beach again. Talk about health and inefficiency.

Shadows were lengthening now, everyone was going in. Seaweed littered the beach like discarded loincloths. Only the fatties were still stretched out. Despite their parasol, they looked somewhat overcooked. Red seals in the sunset.

Rat Race

I am very much looking forward to my first Christmas in Gloucestershire, but wish it would stop raining. An even worse dampener has been put on the proceedings by the prolonged disappearance of the pub cat, which Leo my husband brought down from London on the excuse that it was an early Christmas present. Fazed, no doubt, by the thought of spending Christmas with four neutered toms, she bolted through the cat-door her second morning and went AWOL.

Wednesday
Endlessly comb the surrounding woods and fields looking for cat.

'A fox will have her head off,' says the gardener knowingly, then, seeing my face, hastily adds, 'But don't worry, she'll come back.'

Just hunting desperately for Christmas decorations, which also have gone AWOL in the move, when Stan (the male half of the couple who have come to live with us) gives a shout that the cat's back. Foolishly shrieking with joy, we converge on the hall. 'Terrified by the din, the cat bolts out into the night. Determined to lure her back, we open the cat-door, and leave large plate of chicken beside it.

Thursday
Gratified that the chicken has been eaten – but suspect junior dog is responsible.

Friday
Pub cat, now known as the Lochness Mouser, is sighted near

43

the shed. Rain continues to sweep in great curtains across the valley – I'm dreaming of a wet Christmas.

Saturday
Junior dog rushes in, crackling. Outside we find badgers have raided our dustbins and scattered tins and chicken bones all over the lawn. Clearing it up, Leo sees large rat strolling past. It gives him an old-fashioned look and trips over a Guinness can.

Sunday
Mouse appears on terrace. Leo is so enchanted he fetches it a piece of Brie. I point senior dog's head mousewards, but she looks everywhere except at the offending rodent.

Tuesday
Return from Christmas shopping in London to be greeted by Viv, who says that last night all the water went off, including loos; that the pump is on its last legs; that the washing machine blew her across the room; that the small mouse Leo gave Brie to on the terrace is actually a baby rat and growing fast; and that a hundred rats have moved in under the terrace.

Wednesday
Deeply disappointed by performance of indoor hyacinth bulbs. Their nasty white beaks sticking a quarter inch above the bulb fibre show signs of being nibbled. Try not to contemplate by whom.

Thursday
Gloomily listening to ever-continuing downpour when I hear commotion outside. Find Viv and our two dogs standing on kitchen table, our four cats calmly eating turkey-flavoured Whiskas, as a huge rat saunters across the floor. Join Viv and dogs on table, and give stern pep talk to cats. At this moment two carol singers appear and sheepishly sing 'Silent Night'. Tell them this is singularly inappropriate carol for this house, and overtip.

Following Wednesday
Rats still in evidence. Our gardener tells me the place is infested
44

because all the rats have been flooded out of their holes by the rain. Perhaps they should build a gnawer's ark.

Stay up very late doing Christmas cards. Jump out of my skin at sound of squeaking, but realise it is junior dog having a nightmare.

Go downstairs to lock up, wearing thigh boots, to find our two black tom cats in the hall, saying 'After you, Claude, no, after you, Cecil'. Lying between them is a gigantic twitching rat. Cling on to banisters for support but feel I must put it out of its misery. Box file too light, eventually finish it off with *Collins English Dictionary*, which defines rat as a long-tailed murine rodent.

To think we left London to get away from the rat-race.

Thursday
Council of war at breakfast: no more food to be put out, cat-door to be boarded up. I ring the Council who refer me grandiosely to the Rodent Operative, who promises to come tomorrow. Ring Leo in London, who refuses to take the whole thing seriously, and suggests we put an ad in the village shop for a pied piper.

Sleepless night, listening to rats scurrying, foxes barking, presumably after pub cat, and worrying about the forty-six presents I have yet to buy and whether the turkey will fit into the Aga.

Friday
Temperature dropping fast. Return from village to find Rodent Operative has arrived. A good-looking, winning young man, he refuses all offers of a Christmas drink – perhaps he doesn't want to be a pie-eyed piper – but systematically goes round putting down poison, while Stan boards up all the holes. The Rodent Operative also says we may later need rat deodorant. As it's Christmas why not after-shave as well?

Saturday
Hear foxes barking again all night. Milkman says it is going to snow. Feel I must decorate house and ask gardener why our holly tree doesn't have any berries. As he is explaining it is a male tree which doesn't produce any, we both suddenly see

45

several berries on a top branch and look away hastily.

Just having grisly vision of grinning foxes sitting in the wood warming their ginger paws in front of the fire, while the corpse of the little cat rotates on a spit, when suddenly I hear a blood-curdling scream. Rush downstairs to find Viv in the kitchen, with mascara running down her face.

'What's happened?' I whisper.

'She's come home,' she sobs.

And there was the little cat, terribly thin, raging with temperature but still managing to purr like a jumbo jet in Stan's arms. So it was fatted calves all round. The prodigal cat had returned and for her there was to be no more abiding in the fields. For the first time in ages we all slept like logs.

'Twas the week before Christmas and all through the house not a creature was stirring, not even a rat. And a very merry Christmas from me and the pub cat.

Bally-Awful

I was eighteen when I last went to Majorca, and had a riotous time, dallying with a plumber called Ernesto, and a taxi driver called Juan, before ending up in the muscular arms of a telephone mechanic called Angel.

With such fond memories I was wildly excited when Meon offered us a villa in the north of the island. Leo my husband was not. He abhors the whole idea of the Bally-awful islands, as he calls them, and, sourly opening a file entitled 'Bloody Majorca', gloomily forecast airport strikes, customs hold-ups and drunken tourists being sick into 'Kiss Me Quick' hats.

His sense of outrage increased when he learnt we were flying out on the first day of the test match and, even worse, had a woman pilot. To his intense disappointment, the plane landed on time, the directions across the island were perfect, and the villa – L'Olivar d'Availl – quite ravishing. Like the nicest private house, it had a vast drawing room, five bedrooms, four bathrooms, and sun-trap terraces everywhere.

Even more crucial at 10 p.m. to travellers too weary to go out was a full fridge which included two cooked chickens, cheese and several bottles of wine. At midnight the tiles were still warm on the terrace outside our bedroom. In the garden below cypresses pointed black fingers at huge stars and a full coral pink moon reflected in a swimming pool longer than a cricket pitch.

We were woken by goat bells, cocks crowing and farm dogs barking. Feasting on croissants and apricot jam, I saw two thin stray cats peering down from an olive tree to see if the new arrivals were soft touches. They were. In the supermarket three miles away in Puerto Pollencia, we bought tins of Whiskas 'con sardina'. Leo perked up when he saw Fernet Brancas on special offer, but winced when Emily, my fourteen-year-old daughter, and her friend Catriona who'd come with us, purchased such exotic Majorcan delicacies as baked beans, tomato ketchup and Philadelphia cream cheese.

One great plus was that both children were marvellous at amusing themselves, frolicking like porpoises for hours in the turquoise pool, or devouring Mills and Boon novels with screams of laughter. Further plusses were a sweet villa supervisor who popped in to see we were all right and direct us to the best beaches and restaurants, and a wonderful maid called Maria who made the best paella I'd ever tasted.

Dining out in Majorca is cheap but patchy. We found a good restaurant in Puerto Pollencia called Hibiscus, and another in Cala San Vicente called Mary y P, where you dined under a canopy of ivy. I developed a passion for Rape Soup, a fish stock duster-yellow with saffron and groaning with mussels, prawns and crab claws. Other restaurant outings were less successful. Zarzuela was merely lumps of cod in Brown Windsor, and the grilled squid could have acted as a rubber fetishist's willy-warmer.

We made a few trips to the local beaches: Cala San Vicente, which reeked of sewage; Formentor, by boat, which yielded much to gaze at. Since I last visited the island the women have gone topless, a phenomenon emphasised by the fact that the Majorcans stick their chests out three inches further, whether on land or sea, than any other nation. To avoid being impaled by a massive aquatic brunette, Leo scuttled up the beach.

Mostly we spent our days at the Villa L'Olivar, swimming, sunbathing, watching the dragonflies cruising like Prussian-blue helicopters across the exquisite pool.

By day three we were feeding six cats. Leo, buying ten tins of Whiskas con sardina, was asked by a helpful English tourist if he realised he was buying cat food.

A fat woman glared at me. 'There's that Linda Porter writes for the *Mail*,' she said.

'No it's not,' said her friend. 'It's Gilly Potter.'

Another bonus of the villa was the perfect waste disposal provided by six goats, who survived somehow in a burnt bladeless field next door and who ate everything we gave them including the *Mail on Sunday*. Goat Cuisine, said Leo.

One problem about holidays, if you normally lead a pressured life, is how exhausting it is doing nothing. Nor can I unwind unwined, so I was left with hangovers at dusk and dawn. I had to face the fact too that despite valiant efforts to be jolly, poor Leo was bored out of his skull, not just by the prattle of three teenagers (he includes me) but, because I don't drive, by having to ferry us round on every trip. The children's needs were also different from ours. Having devoured Mills and Boon in the sun all day, they were raring to get off with Sting and Rupert Everett look-alikes in the evening. It was too far for them to walk to Pollencia; anyway we felt they shouldn't be left entirely unchaperoned. But there was no doubt the presence of parents inhibited the hovering Angels and Ernestos, who would have snapped the two girls up as the villa cats pounced on scraps if they'd been alone. Nor do the discos really get going until around two in the morning, by which time, having been woken by assorted cocks at dawn, one was nearly asleep.

By the sixth day, three more cats arrived, and a billy goat, who, despite being hobbled, jumped over a wall, and really enjoyed baked beans and *The Spectator*. The word had obviously got round. In the afternoon a beautiful grey mare and her mule friend trotted up the drive, rushing round scattering hibiscus petals, until an embarrassed owner retrieved them. Perhaps we should start a restaurant called Olivar Cramwell.

Seven in the evening was the witching hour, when the setting sun slanted across olive and almond groves, gilding the pale grasses, warming the parched brown earth, and turning houses and rocks an apricot pink.

We usually drank before dinner on the front at Puerto Pollencia, watching the crowds, the yachts swaying in the harbour, and the lovely soft colours of the windsurfers' sails.

As teenage girls pedalled by on bikes, with boyfriends with skin as smooth and brown as butterscotch standing on the pillion, Emily and Catriona's longing was palpable. Oh Life where is thy Sting!

On the day we left, the weather tactfully went cloudy. Leo, whose bathing trunks had lost their elastic, walked up and down the pool, hands behind his back like Prince Philip to hold them up. The cats all had Falstaffian bellies, the goats finished up everything including *Woman's Own*.

I wished it had been more fun for Leo, but felt, despite a shortage of Angels, the children and I had had a lovely time. We reached Palma airport to find the place in chaos, with all flights hopelessly delayed by a strike. Having lost a fortune trying to ring England, Leo came back with the information that This Was a Major Cock-up, and We Certainly Wouldn't Be Home To-night.

'I say,' whispered Emily. 'Daddy's really really cheered up.'

Not In Front
Of The Children

Mrs Victoria Gillick, that self-appointed custodian of teenage morality, has been on the war-path again, chuntering furiously about parents' wishy-washy attitude to their children's sex-life.

But surely she must heartily approve of children's attitude to their parents' sex life, which is invariably both vigilant and disapproving. Most single parents trying to find a new mate discover they have a Mini-Gillick in the house rotting up any attempt at amorous encounters twenty-four hours a day.

Take my friend Fiona, who is thirty-eight, widowed and very beautiful.

'I have one admirer who rings up occasionally from abroad,' she says. 'Instinctively my two daughters, aged ten and twelve, know it's him and go into an incredible routine of slamming doors and shouting at each other, so I can't hear myself speak. Last week, he took me to Annabel's, the sort of treat I haven't had for years. Next day he dropped in unexpectedly bringing a box of chocolates. Knowing I was frantic for them to behave, the children were appalling, hanging round boot-faced, playing green-eyed gooseberry, constantly referring to my admirer in the third person: "What's HE doing here? When's HE going to go?"'

Normally these are sweet polite children but, having lost one parent, they regard any of their mother's suitors as a threat and play up accordingly.

Added to this antagonism from the Mini-Gillicks, is the astronomical cost of courting for the single parent. One mother, knowing her children will act up if she brings her lover home, spends her entire salary from her part-time job on an all-night baby-sitter twice a week. Others opt for the home fixture, and

51

have all the expense of feeding their lovers. Whereupon the Mini-Gillicks, smelling Boeuf Provençal in the oven and seeing kiwi fruit and out of season strawberries marinading in kirsch in the larder, naturally kick up when they are fobbed off with spaghetti hoops and early bed. Repeatedly the candle-lit dinner will be sabotaged by little faces peering through the bannisters, complaining of sore throats and tummy aches, or embarrassingly demanding why mummy's put freesias on her bedside table.

Away fixtures are often even more traumatic. Take the single parent returning shattered from the office, having to change gear into devoted mother for two hours as she supervises supper and baths. Toenails drying, hair in Carmens, she reads a bedtime story. Then, guiltily shrugging off tearful suffocating hugs that mess up her make-up as she sets off, she has to change gear again into party temptress. Invariably, just as the party's hotting up, and the only attractive man in the room is sidling towards her, she has to bolt home to relieve the baby-sitter. Sometimes she makes the error of smuggling the only attractive man home with her.

'I tried it once,' said a friend sadly. 'Both children, woken by the dog barking, wouldn't go back to sleep. The cat had been sick in the bath. The landing was strewn with toys, and finally he tripped over an un-emptied chamber pot in the bedroom doorway – hardly a lover's bower.'

Nor do locked doors provide one hundred per cent security. Another friend, having ensured her daughter was asleep, bolted herself and her lover, Peregrine, into the dining room. They were just warming up on the Wilton when four-year-old Natasha, apopleptic as any Mr Barrett of Wimpole Street, burst through the hatch, thundering: 'What are you doing to my Mummy?'

To which Peregrine, through gritted teeth, replied: 'Trying to keep her warm.'

It must be a terrifying experience for the child, but not much fun for the lover, particularly when an eighteen-month-old Mini-Gillick with sodden nappy, running nose and ice-cold feet clambers into bed to play chaperone at five in the morning.

One suitor was put off for good after the child burrowed down the bed and, after a pause, emerged, enquiring: 'Why isn't your willy as big as Daddy's?'

But it's not just a question of the child frantically fighting to hang on to his mother. The stumbling block for children of all ages – from J.R. rotting up Miss Ellie's relationship with Clayton to Adrian Mole bristling over his mother's amorous capers – is that they cannot handle their parents' sexuality.

The whole ambiguity is summed up by six-year-old Max, when asked by his mother if he liked her boy friend. 'Yes and No,' he replied. 'I love him when he drives his car fast, but I hate him when he's in your bed.'

Or six-year-old Scarlet, who when told that her mother had died comforted her father that at least he could sell his double bed now, as he wouldn't be needing it anymore.

Textbooks claim that children need time to adjust, that the suitor should make a friend of the children before moving in with the parent. But that doesn't always work. A year later, Scarlet's widowed father met a lovely girl, who played everything by the book, taking Scarlet and her brothers to the zoo, kicking footballs, mending punctures, building snowmen, until they were clamouring for her to move in.

But when she did, Scarlet became quite hysterical and had tantrums for weeks because she discovered her father and the lovely girl were sharing the same bed, not sleeping in separate rooms.

The potential stepmother found it easier to get on with the brothers than with Scarlet. Just as a male suitor can usually cope with a sweet little daughter who clambers on to his knee, but feels threatened by a small boy who is often neurotically bound up with his mother and sees himself as the surrogate husband.

When the children reach adolescence, however, the Mini-Gillicks are more likely to be of the opposite sex. In direct competition with their mothers, they will sabotage the relationship even more ruthlessly. One of the most poignant stories I know concerns a very attractive middle-aged man who fell in love with a widow the same age, and moved in with her very happily. Then her two teenage minxes came home from boarding school, and drifted round the house, bath towels slipping. Unable to handle the pressures, the man moved out.

But is the future that bleak? Is the single parent destined to face the arctic sweep of the double bed alone each night, until she becomes so set in her ways she resents any intruder. She must remember that Mini-Gillicks in the end grow up and leave home, and while respecting that they may feel threatened, she shouldn't kowtow to their bullying and blackmail. Take things slowly, hang on, and remember an awful lot of people make happy second marriages.

Scarlet of the tantrums, for example, has been contentedly living with her father and stepmother for eighteen months now. Natasha, who burst through the hatch, is also happy that Peregrine has been keeping her mother warm at night for three years.

Finally the most touching wedding speech I heard was when the bridegroom beckoned to the bride's seven-year-old son saying with genuine warmth: 'Where's my good friend, Henry, without whose approval this wedding could not have taken place?'

Turn Right
At The Spotted Dog

We have now spent eight long months in this wonderfully hospitable county, but as Nouveau-Rustics, we are still trying to come to terms with the social complications of rural life.

Dining out, for example, is great fun – if you get there. There's no *A–Z* in Gloucestershire. Most people are too grand to put names outside their houses, and my rusty shorthand is quite incapable of getting down those rattled-off instructions: 'You turn right at the Spotted Dog, then you come to a *hideous* modern bungalow – well that's not us . . .'

The result is blazing rows on the way to every party, with Leo careering round the same perilous country lanes saying he's bloody going home, and me, tearfully envisaging no dinner and social ostracisation, saying: 'I'm sure they said left at the Spotted Dog.'

In the end we always have to ask. It must be hell being a yokel in Gloucestershire. Every Saturday your evening viewing is interrupted by twerps in dinner jackets saying: 'Can you possibly tell me the way to the Smith-Binghams?'

The chief problem, however, for the Nouveau-Rustic is sartorial. In London it never mattered what I wore. Here I get it wrong every time. The first dinner party we went to was very grand. I rolled up in high heels, a knee-length velvet skirt and a pleated satin shirt (which had pleats going both ways after twenty miles under a seat belt) to find my hostess in pink cords and a Guernsey sweater.

On my second jaunt, Leo was away. I was invited this time for supper in the kitchen. Natch, I put on cords and a jersey, to be greeted by a vast dinner party, the men in dark suits, the women in silk shirts and velvet skirts, all the silver on the dining room table, and – most un-London of all – a spare man for me who wasn't queer.

The next invitation said 'black tie'. So I deduced we should dress up this time. Alas, the week before, Leo split his dinner jacket trousers at some binge in London, and borrowed a pair from a friend of six foot six. Consequently his cummerbund had to be tied under his armpits like the top half of a strapless bikini. He also found a large wine mark on the lapel of his white dinner jacket, and covered it with an *Animals in War* badge. I wore a long black dress, which plunged to the navel.

We arrived to find all the women very covered up, mostly in short wool dresses, several of the men without ties, and our host wearing green cords, an old green coat, a blue striped shirt, a green bow tie and brown suede shoes.

As the evening sun slanted cruelly on Leo's white dinner jacket and my over-exposed, middle-aged bosom, we felt like two Crufts poodles with pompom tails and *diamanté* collars let loose at a rough shoot. Happily it turned out a marvellous evening, with poodles and gundogs frisking merrily together – and, unlike London, no one talked about house prices or education. And that's another thing, never ask men in the country what they do for a living. Very few of them seem to do anything.

I also notice that it's the drawing room tables who seem to wear the long skirts down here, and everyone covers up not only their bosoms but also their plant pots – with flowered vases called cache-pots. Perhaps I should wear a cache-pot to the next party.

But having received all this lovely hospitality, we now have to pay it back. In London we never gave dinner parties. During the week we were knackered, and at the weekend everyone pushed off to the country, and anyway we'd got nothing to give them with.

Consequently, when we had our first dinner party in Gloucestershire, we had to go out and buy three sets of plates, three sets of glasses, knives, table mats, even napkins. Kitchen roll – like patriotism – is not enough.

The party was a moderate success. The paté tasted of blendered thermal underwear, the pudding of uncooked marmalade. But the venison produced by Leo and my
56

housekeeper Viv was brilliant. The guests included two local landowners and their wives, a couple who weekend down here and their house guests, who turned out to be a boilermaker from Stockport and his wife.

There was a sticky moment when the boilermaker announced to the straighter of the landowners that he always kissed his son on the mouth when they met.

'How old is your boy?' asked the landowner.

'Twenty-seven,' said the boilermaker.

And a riotous moment when the boilermaker's wife asked Leo how he'd cooked the venison, whereupon Stan, my housekeeper's husband – who was serving the pudding – proceeded to tell her. Five minutes later, despite vicious kicks on the ankle from Viv and nine people unserved, the venison hadn't even reached the oven but was still being larded with green bacon and garlic pellets.

No one appeared to drink too much. But after saying goodbye to everyone, I found Leo crawling round the kitchen pretending to be an outside labrador, and Stan sleeping peacefully on the landing.

And now summer is here I am getting nervous about the garden. When people come to dinner, it's still light and they can gaze out of the window on the crimes, as Nouveau-Rustics, we've already committed: planting poplars, which obscure a view, or, even more heinous, putting in strident colours.

'Never have red in a Cotswold garden,' my neighbour told me the other night. 'Pink, blue, yellow, silver and, best of all, white, and do plant your clumps in odd numbers.' And I prayed that my two newly installed red-hot pokers wouldn't suddenly let me down by flashing at her over the terrace wall. But to prove her point, the local nursery told me that recently Princess Michael completely denuded them of plants – but only white ones. It's better to be dead than red in a Gloucestershire garden.

But we're getting on very well. Last week we gave our second dinner party. Among the guests were the new Lord and his wife, who moved into the village even more recently than we did. Viv got so carried away she took the afternoon off to have her hair put up, and wore her wedding dress. The new Lord, perhaps feeling that this was what an aristocrat should wear to dine with the literati, rolled up very handsome in a Fair Isle jersey and one of those hairy tweed coats heroines bury their faces in at the end of romantic novels.

In fact local interest has been slightly diverted away from this New Lord on to an even newer Lord, who's just moved into the next door village and who dropped in on Monday to warn us that his new sheep had jumped out of their field and been chasing dogs all over the valley all the weekend.

He was another surprise. I always thought people who kept sheep wore dung-coloured clothes to blend into the countryside, but he turned up in a pink polo-necked jersey and tartan trousers. Not unlike my very good friend and social adviser, the milkman, who raised two fingers to massive Tory bias on polling day, going on his rounds in a scarlet sweater and a red check shirt. I nearly asked him to stand in the garden beside my two red-hot pokers and form an odd-numbered clump.

The answer, of course, is not to care what anyone thinks and be yourself. But I'm not sure who myself is. I went to a party recently in the London house immortalised last month when Anna Ford chucked a glass of wine in the face of her ex-boss Jonathan Aitken. As I entered the room, my hostess advanced towards me smiling: 'Hullo Polly,' she said.

When Daddy
Came Marching Home

Victory in Europe – forty years later, the three words still bring a lump to my throat and make the hairs on the back of my neck prickle with excitement. But it is difficult for anyone to appreciate the euphoria and colossal sense of achievement we felt on VE Day, unless they realise the gruelling hardship people endured in Britain throughout the war.

Not that it was hard for me. Only two when war began, I had never known anything else. My first hazy memories were of my father going off to fight in France in 1939, and my mother, my brother Timothy, my Nanny, Jamie our Scottish terrier and about forty-five teddy bears making a nightmare fourteen-hour journey up to Yorkshire to stay with an aunt.

There was no heating on the train, no lights and no food. We wolfed our dried egg sandwiches in the first half hour, and the queues were so long at all the station buffets that my mother never dared buy any food in case the train moved on. As night fell, she kept opening the blackout curtains a fraction, desperate that we might have passed our destination as unlit stations flashed by.

I clearly remember her singing at the top of her voice when, after weeks of frantic uncertainty, a telegram arrived saying my father was safe home from Dunkirk. She was so excited she weeded half my aunt's garden. The syringa was in bloom. Even today if I breathe in its sweet heady smell, it triggers off instant euphoria.

I remember my mother disappearing into a great bear hug when she met my father at Leeds the next day. She expected him to be haggard, but he had never looked better: tanned almost black by the French sun and sea air, and two stone

59

lighter from not eating.

A reticent, modest man, he talked little about the ordeal. One of his friends and fellow officers in France was the champion shot at Bisley. When my father and he and a party of soldiers were creeping towards Dunkirk, a German tank appeared on the horizon more than two thousand yards away. Through binoculars, they saw the turret open and a German officer pop his head out. Casually, as though there was absolutely no danger from the British, he lit a cigarette. Egged on by my father, the Bisley champion borrowed a rifle from one of the men and, incredibly, picked the German off.

'We couldn't stand his damn nonchalance,' was my father's only comment.

Nor did he dwell on the horrors of Dunkirk, except to describe one ludicrous incident. Waiting endlessly for a little boat, he suddenly noticed the rocks were covered in tar and instinctively, despite bombs and bullets falling round him, removed his tin hat and sat on it, so his trousers wouldn't get dirty.

Happily, on his return, he was posted to the Staff College, and we went to live in Camberley. Here we all carried gas masks which we never used, and identity disks were attached to our wrists with our names, addresses and telephone numbers on.

Then occurred my worst tragedy of the war. My adored brother Timothy, then aged seven, was sent away to prep school. To my mother's distress at his departure was added dismay when an irate neighbour rang up saying: 'Please come and fetch Timothy, he's been crying on my doorstep for the past three days.'

Frantic that my brother had run away from school, my mother tore round, only to find our Scottie, Jamie, to whose collar Timothy's old identity disk had been transferred, sitting outside the house whining after the neighbour's bitch.

In 1941, my father went to the War Office, and we moved, till the end of the war, to Cobham. A sleepy and in those days very rural Surrey suburb, it had a winding river, a village green and white pebbledash houses with red roofs and leaded windows, the gardens of which were hidden from the outside world by great ramparts of rhododendrons.

Cobham's tranquillity was an illusion. By night the Tarter

Hill Guns pounded away, the village was blacked out except for a huddle of searchlights scraping the sky like rapiers, the sirens howled, and the whole family including Jamie would seek refuge in the broom cupboard under the stairs.

Having known nothing else, I didn't realise how short of food we were, probably because my mother, who never weighed more than seven stone throughout the war, gave me most of her rations. I remember eating delicious spinach, which was in fact nettles, and making my weekly treat of a boiled egg last for at least six pieces of bread. Because fat was so short, my mother mixed butter and marge, but never resorted, as some did, to making cakes with liquid paraffin.

The greatest excitement of the war for us was when my father went to Portugal and leased a group of islands called the Azores (so that the Germans couldn't have them), and also brought back the first orange I had ever tasted. On a mission later to America, he returned with my first ever banana, and longed-for lipstick and silk stockings for my mother.

The best thing about Portugal, said my father, was seeing all the lights on. The blackout in England was horrible, menacing – like having a thick blanket thrown over one's head whenever one ventured outside. One night when my mother was in hospital with pneumonia, my father picked me up from the people opposite when he got home. Crossing our road in inky blackness, he tripped over a paving stone and dropped me, breaking my arm.

Far worse than the blackout or the lack of food was the cold, as we queued endlessly in the bitter winters that characterised the war. I had terrible chilblains. A friend says that the thing he remembers about my mother were her little blue hands. It seemed almost colder indoors than outside, our only heating being a small coal fire in the drawing room.

My mother was appointed Road Mother, which meant she had to keep our bath filled with water (which often froze) at all times, in case the air-raid warden opposite needed to extinguish anything. In fact, the only thing he needed to extinguish in our road were the fires of extra-marital passion.

Only years after did I learn that Mrs B, who was always so bravely cheerful despite a husband away in the Navy, had a lover who stealthily arrived after the blackout. Or that Mrs X and Mr Y, who were always joking and gave me their sweet ration, and whom I so preferred to their grouchy other halves, had actually fallen in love fire-watching and carried on a raging affair throughout the war.

Everyone bicycled everywhere. If anyone came to stay, my father went to the station, riding his own bike and guiding my brother's, which had a wonky seat that tipped backwards. When one aunt arrived, all we could see was her nervous little face peering just above the handlebars.

There were few cars on the road, and no signposts. Leatherhead, four miles away but unvisited, seemed like Africa. In this curiously enclosed world, people seldom went out at night. We made our own amusements, singing round the piano. How the pop songs 'Run, Rabbit, Run' and 'Hey Little Hen' lifted our spirits!

Clothes being so short, I was lucky my mother was good at sewing, and made most of mine. For my sixth birthday party, all the children invited had a going-away present of a little horse made from an old brown blanket, each with a mane and tail of different coloured wool.

As the bombs got worse, my parents installed a Morrison shelter. A huge, ugly, green metal table with wiremesh sides, it only left space in the dining room for one narrow single bed. This my parents shared, stretched out like two anchovies in a tin, for the rest of the war. At the first wail of the siren, they rolled into the shelter beside Jamie and me. Goodness knows what it did to their sex lives. Perhaps that was why I was their last child.

For me, it was a fantastic comfort having them so near, racked as I was by fearful nightmares of German parachutists disguised as nuns, the Gestapo tugging out my finger nails, and Japs with slit eyes sidling through the bamboo shoots, filling me up with water and jumping on my stomach.

My attitudes were very simple. The French were soppy dates because they had caved in. Monty was a star who turned the war. The Americans were also stars, because they threw me chewing-gum out of passing tanks, until I overheard my father telling a chum that Ike had a mistress. I was appalled. A mistress meant a schoolteacher. How soppy of the Americans to need a teacher to tell them how to fight. Our generals could do it on their own.

It is impossible to describe the adulation we felt for the cuddly, jaunty, defiant figure of Mr Churchill; at times the glowing red tip of his cigar seemed the only thing that lightened our darkness. Hitler was of course the arch-fiend, the focus of all loathing.

'Did we really detest him that much?' I asked my mother the other day.

'Oh yes,' she thought for a minute. 'Even more than Mr Scargill.'

D-Day raised everyone's hopes. Over the fence, I heard people saying war would be over by Christmas. I was thrilled my father had promised me a pony.

But the mood of optimism was shattered by the arrival of the doodlebugs which terrorised southern England. One fell as we were about to bathe in the river. Hearing the throbbing overhead like some malignant flying taxi, we all flattened in the wild garlic, except two of my little friends, who prostrated themselves in the one bed of nettles not yet turned into spinach, which caused more tears than the subsequent explosion.

Another bomb fell on our school. All the windows blew in, filling the orange jelly we were eating for pudding with lethal splinters. Within minutes, hoards of ashen mothers converged from all sides, like the Valkyries, peddling furiously. Fortunately none of us was hurt. School on the other hand was closed for two months – my first inkling that Hitler might be on my side.

My father was a brigadier now, one of the youngest in the army. I nearly burst with pride each morning as I saw him stride off down the road with a red band on his hat. But for my mother, he left home six days a week for bomb-torn London, and was never back until after nine at night. Considering how many fathers were away fighting or in staff jobs, most children were brought up in virtually one-parent families. As the war entered its sixth year, the strain began to tell, mothers got rattier, staff at school more bad-tempered.

Then at long last on 7 May 1945, as my mother was bashing the stems of some wisteria, we heard on the wireless that the Germans had surrendered.

'Pinch me,' she said. 'So I know I'm awake.'

Why was she crying? She'd never cried before except when Jamie was put down. Had we lost after all? Then she laughed and dried her eyes on her apron, and we ran into the street. People were cheering and hugging, and hanging out flags, a little crumpled after five years in the attic. Then suddenly the bells rang out, peeling gloriously from Cobham, Oxshott and Leatherhead, echoing across the flat black-earthed Surrey landscape, announcing the fall of the powers of darkness.

My father took May 8th off. My brother came home from prep school. Together in the kitchen we listened to Mr Churchill's bulldog growl: 'The evil-doers now lie prostrate before us. Advance Britannia,' followed by cheer upon cheer.

We had a great party in the evening at one of the big houses on the hill. I had a bath beforehand and, used to washing with only a sliver as thin as a communion wafer, was amazed my mother didn't scold me for leaving a new bar of pink soap in the water.

The weather was muggy and warm. Carrying a red jelly and a shepherd's pie containing our entire week's meat ration, we walked to the party. Every house was ablaze with lights and strewn with union jacks and bunting. The scent of lilacs and the Badedas tang of nearby pine woods mingled with the smell of hundreds of bonfires and beacons turning the sky to rose.

Reaching the party, we found bunting hung from lights all round the garden. The women looked lovely in their cotton dresses – one enterprising lady had even run up a long skirt from her blackout curtains. But my mother, as always, seemed loveliest in a green flowered dress which matched her eyes.

Drifting around was old Lady Thornley, a legend in Cobham since she emerged unhurt from the drawing room after a direct hit on her house, and her husband, seeing her white hair totally blacked with soot, said gallantly: 'My dear, you look twenty years younger.'

I was madly in love with our host, who went up to London every day in a black coat with an astrakhan collar, and who seemed able to get masses of everything from gin to milk chocolate throughout the war. The tables certainly groaned with food – jellies, jam tarts, spam and corned beef, even a nobly sacrificed chicken. There also seemed buckets to drink.

The host's father-in-law, a knight very high up in the Civil

Service, was a great character. Running around in pre-war gym shoes, with holes cut out for his corns, he supervised the huge bonfire, which reared up nearly twelve feet tall at the bottom of the garden. Perched on top was an effigy of Hitler with mad staring eyes, slicked black hair, a little black moustache and Swastika armbands. At last the great pyre roared into golden flame. After two thousand days of blackout, the brilliance was breathtaking. Birds disturbed by the unaccustomed brightness sang their heads off. Insects freaked out, moths bashing against the lights, colossal maybugs bombing us like doodlebugs.

Looking across the garden my mother suddenly stiffened. For there was my father laughing and shoving his hand down a blonde's dress. But it was only old Lady Thornley again. This time her white hair was turned gold by the bonfire, and my father was retrieving a maybug from her cleavage.

Later we toasted Mr Churchill and the King and Queen, and there was singing. My favourite song, written by Hubert Gregg, was about getting 'lit-up when the lights go up in London'. 'The whole population will be canned, canned, canned', went one verse. 'Through our gins and Angosturas, we'll see little pale pink Fuehrers Hi de Heiling from the Circus in the Strand.'

Then we bellowed out 'There'll always be an England', and all the grown-ups cried. Really they seemed an awfully soppy bunch.

My poor brother remembers having the most excruciating earache that night, and no one taking any notice because they were all plastered. I got awful indigestion from eating half-raw baked potatoes with charred outsides from the bonfire. My best friend guzzled a whole tin of condensed milk, and was sick in the rhododendrons.

But the Tarter Hill guns were silent, as half asleep we were carried somewhat unsteadily home by my parents. Gradually it sank in that we had won the war, and we were free.

My father had made us a see-saw for Christmas 1944, which not only went up and down but round and round. It was such an amazing novelty that our garden was always packed with excited, yelling children, fighting for a turn. The see-saw had a hollow base, with a hole in it. Putting his hand inside to tighten the screw the morning after VE Day, my father was amazed to find a blue tit sitting on four eggs, which she later hatched out. Despite all the yelling, the fighting, the bombs and the pounding guns, she had determinedly stuck to her post and raised her family. Just as the British, despite the terrors and hardships, had finally won through. She seemed to symbolise our war.

TWO

Portrait Gallery

Neil Kinnock

This piece appeared in September 1983 on the eve of the Labour Party Conference, at which Neil Kinnock became leader. His remarks about other members of the party, particularly Meacher, Benn and Wilson, were picked up by all the other Sundays, and the Mail on Sunday *led on the story. By midday Mr Kinnock had denied making any of the remarks, but fortunately they were all down in my notebook.*

Neil Kinnock not only cares – but more important he has to be seen to care. When I first met him three years ago in the Commons, he was so busy hailing fellow MPs, chatting up a party of blind men, and pumping visiting pensioners by the hand, it was almost impossible to get a word in edgeways.

This week in the South Wales colliery town of Pontllanfraith, it was the same. Arriving at his house, I found a bright scarlet front door, no bell and no Neil. Soon I was joined by a handsome man and his springer spaniel, who with its ginger ears, freckled paws and indiscriminate amiability was not unlike Mr Kinnock.

'Waiting for Neil are you?' asked the handsome man, who turned out to be the local youth officer. 'He's a great bloke, cares about the area, people love him round here, he remembers their names.'

'Would he remember to turn up?' I asked anxiously as it started to rain.

'Oh yes, he's always late.'

If you have charm, people will wait for you. As several other people stopped to pass the time of day and sing our Neil's praises, I realised Mr Kinnock's warmth is very much a local trait.

And suddenly he drove up in the blue Rover the TGWU have given him to replace the Ford he piled up on the M4. Two weeks holiday in Tuscany had bleached the Tabasco red hair and given him a tan which blended into the freckles. Bouncing out, weighed down by a duvet, two carrier bags and an overweight briefcase, he said we couldn't get in because he'd forgotten the key, but D'reen up the road had a spare.

'How was Strasbourg?' I began, but Mr Kinnock was already pumping the youth officer by the hand, telling him to Give us a Shout if he needed anything.

'How,' I began again, but our Neil had bounded into the traffic, across the road to shake hands with an ancient constituent and disappear inside his house. Ten minutes later he was back. The poor old boy's wife had died recently.

In between waving at passers-by, he tried to light his pipe, but gave up because of the rain which was now sweeping symbolically rightwards. I asked him about his U-turn on the Common Market.

'The British don't like the Common Market,' he replied. 'But they're wrongly frightened we couldn't survive without it. It's like saying I can't give up booze because I might freeze to death'.

'I was addressing the Socialist group over there,' he went on, then added in outraged tones, as though he'd never done the same thing himself, 'and in the middle two Frenchmen started talking. I told them to shut up.'

By now we were quite wet, so I was relieved when D'reen arrived with the key. The house inside was delightful and blissfully warm. The knocked-through room contains a pine table and a Welsh dresser. On the walls are Lowry prints, numerous photographs of Mr Kinnock's wife Glenys and their two children, a framed *Private Eye* cover featuring Mr Kinnock and Mr Foot, and a certificate to show Mr Kinnock had been down a mine.

Mr Kinnock apologised for the Venetian blinds – without them he'd never get any peace – and offered me real or instant coffee.

'Instant's fine,' I said.

'Real coffee's much nicer.'

'Isn't it rather middle class?' I said, teasing.

'No,' Mr Kinnock bridled. 'The Italian working classes wouldn't dream of drinking anything but real coffee.'

Wasn't he thrilled about becoming leader?

Just for a second he dropped his guard, grinning engagingly from ear to ear. Then remembering his image as the caring family man who's unwittingly had a greatness thrust upon him, added 'But at forty-one, I'm too young. The kids are at the wrong age, Rachel's eleven, Stevie's thirteen. Before entering the leadership stakes, I had to think very seriously whether such a commitment would damage the kids.'

Were they impressed?

'Not very,' said Mr Kinnock, adding skimmed milk to his coffee. 'Although I've become an excellent source of autographs for Rachel. Stevie'd be more impressed if I captained Wales.'

Neil Kinnock is shrewd enough to realise this may be the last chance for the Labour Party, that unless they clean up their act and present some appearance of unity, they'll never win another election.

How would he tackle the problem?

'Left, right and centre of the party have only to observe one discipline, the self-discipline of the will to win. To those who won't realise this, who insist on short-term squabbles, who'd rather fight ally than enemy, I'll give no quarter. I'm not asking them to make terrific sacrifices, just to think before they open their mouths. Bloody blinds,' he leapt restlessly to his feet to adjust them.

Evidently at the TUC conference, he'd commuted between Unions, urging them to boot out their militants. Wouldn't there be a backlash?

'People overemphasise the militant danger,' said Mr Kinnock. 'They're terrified of Meacher, they regard him as Benn's vicar on earth, and use his name to frighten their children. In reality, he's kind, scholarly, innocuous – and as weak as hell.'

Obviously thinking Hattersley would be elected to the deputy leadership, Mr Kinnock described him as 'a nice man'.

'Nice,' I said incredulously.

'I can work with him,' said Mr Kinnock firmly, which means the same thing.

Tony Benn however was dismissed as a spent force.

'Couldn't knock the skin off a rice pudding.'

Was it true he had once described Benn as a blind worm trying to be an adder? For a second Mr Kinnock flickered between discretion and the desire to be credited with a bon mot. He opted for the former, saying: 'Attribute that to me, and I'll kill you.'

He has a good face, and, as with most people with charm, it gets more attractive the longer you look at it. Despite reports to the contrary he still has lots of hair, but as he is small – five foot five at the most – people tend to look down on the bald patch. Then there's the voice, husky and distractingly seductive, which makes everything he says sound wonderfully significant, until you analyse it afterwards.

People accuse Kinnock of laziness. He is assiduous at promoting his own image, making speeches round the country, but less anxious about buckling down to the donkey work of dissecting white papers. It is also said he is not very bright. He failed his degree the first time at Cardiff – not a very academic university. But then being an intellectual didn't get Mr Foot very far. According to Saatchi and Saatchi, even before the election Kinnock was the man the Tories feared most because he offered a street brightness which appealed to the voter.

What did he feel about the beauty contest set up between David Owen, David Steel and himself, all youngish, attractive and wooing the middle classes?

Mr Kinnock laughed. 'I'm bound to lose on the beauty stakes, but I'm not after the female vote, I'm after everyone.'

He agreed that the word 'middle class' had somehow shifted to embrace everyone in work. 'It's given them a terrible self-righteousness. Mrs Thatcher has made them look down on people who haven't got jobs. But forget the glamour,' he went on, becoming positively Churchillian, 'we've got a product to sell, we're not a record sleeve party like the SDP.'

He doesn't like David Owen much either.

'He's intelligent, anyone can be intelligent. What we need in politics is common sense. And the man's arrogant, orthopaedically arrogant in every pore,' which once again sounds splendid when delivered with the Welsh ring of confidence, until you get home and look up 'orthopaedic', to discover it means curing deformities of the bone, and realise the

72

phrase is meaningless.

Nor did he like the media's latest interpretation of him as the thinking man's Harold Wilson.

'Harold Wilson's a petty bourgeois and will remain so in spirit, even if they make him a viscount,' he snapped. For someone who intends to scourge the party of sniping, Mr Kinnock's pretty high in the vitriol stakes himself.

Kinnock was born in March 1942, and came from a happy, united family. His father was a miner, later a steel worker, his mother a district nurse. Although both parents worked, and money can't have been short, they made a decision to have only one child, so all their resources and time could be devoted to Neil. Both sadly died when he was twenty-nine.

Wasn't he heartbroken that they weren't alive to witness his success?

'I am,' said Mr Kinnock wistfully, then once again remembering his image as the caring parent, hastily added, 'But it hurts far more that they never knew the kids.'

Kinnock first met his wife Glenys, who teaches backward children, when they were both at Cardiff University.

'Was it love at first sight?'

'Not quite so elevated as that.'

'Lust then?'

Mr Kinnock shot me a calculating look, as though trying to assess my age.

'Even when one's young,' he said winningly, 'one only lusts after women in their forties, or perhaps thirties,' he went on quickly, thinking he might have overshot the mark.

People who know the Kinnocks well say the dashing and rather beautiful Mrs Kinnock is the power behind the throne. She believes in the Welsh tradition of women living through their men and driving them on.

'Would the real cabinet decisions be taken at home?' I asked.

Mr Kinnock denied this with rather too much conviction.

'No, no, but I value the woman's opinions, she's so bright, and she has a quite uncanny, basic sense of justice, she knows what's right. She always counsels caution. If you do that, she tells me, you'll only get into trouble. I try to heed her, it doesn't always work. She buys all my clothes, even my suits. I don't know how she copes with me and the children and her job, but

73

she's like the great footballers, she's always got time.'

Mrs Kinnock won't give interviews, because it takes the limelight off her husband, and also, allegedly, because she's terrified of putting her foot in it. At the time of the Royal Wedding, however, she talked to a newspaper, saying: 'We were asked to the wedding, but we weren't in the least interested, and of course we didn't go.'

According to Kinnock, his wife was misquoted. She wanted to talk about education and politics, and the interviewer kept rabbiting on about the wedding until Mrs Kinnock was goaded into saying they weren't interested.

'Weren't you?' I asked.

'No,' said Mr Kinnock.

'Didn't you watch on telly?'

'No,' the green eyes flicker, then go opaque when he doesn't like a subject.

'None of you?'

'No – well, Glenys and Rachel watched some of it,' he admitted. 'But then Rachel's very into being a bridesmaid,' as though that justified such a monarchist lapse.

Actually, went on Mr Kinnock, trimming, he liked the Queen, and Charles was a nice old bumbler.

'When I was in Strasbourg,' he added, trimming further, 'and that Greek idiot was sounding off about the Russians shooting down that plane, I thought thank God we've got a queen with dignity, who keeps her nose out of politics.'

Mr Kinnock is spoken of as the Messiah who will lead the Labour Party into the promised land. Whether the land will be as promised is debatable. He's already fudging on the Common Market and Polaris. But at least there will be no U-turn over the abolition of the private schools. Mr Kinnock is out for their blood. The first year in power, he will make parents pay VAT on school fees. The next, fee-paying will be made illegal.

'I believe in nurturing parents,' said Mr Kinnock sanctimoniously. 'But if I give my kids as much help as I can, it doesn't affect the other children. But because of the status attached to the independent schools, it makes the maintained sector feel inferior – and they attach far too much importance to academic achievement. What we need,' he went on, warming to his subject, 'is intelligence,' then, remembering he'd

74

attacked Dr Owen for the same quality, 'or rather common sense.'

Wasn't it totalitarianism to forbid parents to educate their children as they wished? Britain would be the only country in the free world to do so.

'Britain', replied Mr Kinnock heavily, 'is the only country so divided by class.'

'It'll cause a frightful row.'

'I like rows,' said Mr Kinnock, radiating egalitarian spite.

Things were getting a bit frosty, so I asked Mr Kinnock how he unwound.

'By being with the children. I came back knackered from Strasbourg, and helped Rachel with her fractions.'

One would think he was pitching for a job running a children's home rather than the leadership of the Labour Party.

How had he coped when he'd lost his voice?

Just for one second, again unable to resist a joke, he dropped his guard and became human again: 'Oh home life picked up dramatically. I wasn't able to shout at the kids.'

On the way home, I tried to work out how I felt. You can't help liking Neil Kinnock, as a man devoted to his family with a genuine desire to help those in need. With the leadership only a few days away, he is also obviously proceeding like a batsman on 99, determined not to say anything to rock the boat. Why then do I suspect him of ruthless ambition, calculation and extreme deviousness? Perhaps because these qualities are necessary in a successful politician, particularly one who is going to unite the Labour Party. It is sad that the mantle of power is already turning into a straitjacket.

David Gower

This piece was written in August 1983 before David Gower was made captain of England. Meeting him, I felt he had all the right qualities. History proved me wrong. He is probably too nice, but is just as much, if not more, value to the English side as a great batsman.

'New Year's Eve, Sydney,' wrote the teenage daughter of a cricket correspondent in her 1983 diary. 'At midnight as the fireworks went off, David Gower kissed me on the cheek – the year can only deteriorate from now on.'

David Gower has that effect on people. He has the androgynous beauty that appeals to both sexes, curls as blond as the bleached Lord's pitch, a puckish grin, and extraordinary eyes with their huge expanse of white below the dark blue iris. Despite the delicate features of Bubbles in the Pears Soap advertisement, he is macho enough to bat without a helmet, so there is only the blond curls and the perfect timing between him and death. How many female fans must have clasped their hands to their mouths on Thursday when he ducked into a short-pitched ball? And how many hearts fluttered with admiration as he battled on, still refusing the helmet.

Despite the female adulation and even the most hardened cricket correspondents writing about his batting as though they've been kissed under the mistletoe, he has remained unspoilt. He had the good manners to answer my request for an interview by return of post in longhand. Although asked to, he didn't reverse the charges when he rang long distance to arrange dinner. He was waiting in the hotel lobby when I arrived and promptly bought me a large drink.

Later at dinner, he toyed with duck – perhaps an unhappy

choice for a batsman – and downed a whole bottle of champagne without, regrettably, letting a single indiscretion fall from his perfectly formed lips. Like a yellow labrador whose master has been posted away to Germany, he is friendly but detached. Tim Rice who knows him well says he's very shy.

If you bred sportsmen, like racehorses, David Gower would have the ideal pedigree. The branches of his family tree are weighed down with hurdlers, lacrosse and hockey internationals, cricket and croquet players. A Monday's child – appropriately fair of face – he was born on April Fool's Day 1957, in Tonbridge, while his father, who was in the colonial service, was on leave. Although Gower has the placid, passive amiability of the baby of a large family, he was, in fact, an only child. Packed off to prep school at eight, he not only excelled at games but was exceptionally bright, later getting a scholarship to King's, Canterbury, where he ended up with nine O-levels and three A-levels, with a distinction in history.

His first real setback was at fifteen when his father, whom he adored, died of the terribly wasting illness, Hodgkin's disease. The second was failing to get into Oxford. 'I answered a question on King Arthur, whom I knew nothing about. The result was pure regurgitated *Camelot*.' Instead he read law at London University, which bored him to death. He lasted two terms, then to his mother's horror – she wanted him to get a degree first – he fled academic life to play cricket for Leicester. 'I kicked off in the worst possible way, turning up for my first day's training in a dark suit.'

He was knocked into shape by that hardest of taskmasters, Ray Illingworth, who realised Gower's genius would only succeed if he learned to apply it. Despite continual badgering from Illy, affection and respect grew between the two men. Reacting to the fiasco with the dark suit, Gower irritated Illingworth by dressing sloppily. One morning to tease him Gower came down to breakfast in a dinner jacket. Illingworth, however, had the last word. 'Just come in, Gower?' he said acidly.

This tough initiation stood Gower in good stead. Seven years later, he has 52 Test matches, 3,000 Test runs and the vice-captaincy of England under his belt, and is estimated to be capable of making £100,000 a year. He gets a huge fan mail, but is modestly quick to point out that not all of it is complimentary. Someone recently sent him a cutting from an Australian newspaper with a headline: 'Gower Flashes to Hogg'. Underneath they had written one word: 'Numbskull'.

He speaks ruefully of his one lapse in seven years of impeccable cricketing behaviour. In New Zealand this year, at the end of a punishing four and three-quarter months' tour, he was batting when drunks invaded the pitch.

'I told one to go away four times, but he kept on coming. Suddenly the fuse blew. I grabbed him round the neck and frog-marched him off. I got a letter from him later in the year, brought over by one of the New Zealand scorers.'

'Was he apologetic?' I asked. Gower laughed: 'No, abusive. He said I was entirely responsible for him now having a police record.'

A staunch Tory, who does the *Daily Telegraph* crossword every day, Gower is always ready to tell a story against himself. He was recently invited to a party at Downing Street. 'Denis was very friendly and offered me a bite of gin, but Mrs Thatcher, despite her flashing teeth, didn't know me from Adam…. The other day, I was asked to open a local gas board showroom. To send them up gently, I rolled up in a T-shirt of Snoopy lying in his kennel, saying: "I believe in conserving energy". In fact it was a total bomb. Only five housewives turned up, and none of them had a clue who I was.'

One reason perhaps Gower is able to laugh at himself is that for the past five years he has had the same enchanting girlfriend, Vicki Stewart, who obviously cherishes him and comforts him if he is down, but teases him unmercifully and bursts his bubbles if there is any sign of uppishness. Sadly for his female admirers, she is exceptionally pretty, with hair the colour of French mustard, a magnificent tan speckled with freckles, and large, wary, aquamarine eyes. She and Gower live together in a house in Leicester with three goldfish named Eric, and an adopted stray cat called Brian because he stayed close. Gower, according to Vicki, is not domesticated. He hasn't hoovered for two years, but he can make 'deflated omelettes' and does his own packing.

Like many cricketers he is highly superstitious. 'If you made a hundred last time, you search frantically round for the same left sock, right sock, knickers, box, jockstrap and trousers to

78

bring you luck this time. Then you get a duck, and try out a completely different combination next time.'

Gower, something of a dandy on and off the field, is scathing about the official England touring uniform: 'There's never time for fittings, so we all go round like a team of Wombles in baggy trousers and flapping blazers.'

David and Vicki are under constant pressure from the media, who can't believe that today's young can live together happily without necessarily needing the security of marriage and who are always proposing to David on Vicki's behalf.

'One paper wrote something so vile the other day,' she said, 'I went straight to the loo and threw up.'

But on the whole the relationship is tender and sunny. When Gower went down to the Lord's Test two days before Vicki, she bet him he wouldn't dare walk into the hotel alone carrying a pile of her dresses. On the way in, he was barracked by an idling group of taxi drivers, and promptly cracked back: 'You should see the matching handbags I've got for each dress, dearie.'

It is this easy-going nonchalance, coupled with the exquisite, apparent effortlessness of his batting, that makes some people doubt his depth of character. He has been vice-captain for more than a year – the Gower behind the throne. But is he heavyweight enough to lead the side? Gower himself is edgy on the subject. He has got his batting together, he has learnt concentration, and insists he could do the job: 'You needn't be a bastard to be a good captain – just firm. And as a non-bowling captain I'm far more likely to be objective on the field.'

Since the South African ban, with so few good batsmen around, the selectors are probably terrified Gower would lose form with authority. Tony Lewis, the cricket writer, disagrees with this. Gower, he says, has the ability to make people do what he wants without being aggressive, and like Red Rum, he rises better to the bigger challenge.

His horoscope indicates both astonishing powers of leadership and generosity of spirit. The latter comes out in his latest book *Heroes and Contemporaries*, to be published in October, where he displays a wisdom and understanding of his colleagues way beyond his years. So one is treated to views of Willis stoically enduring red-hot needles through his toenails to drain off blood blisters after the day's bowling; or of Rodney Marsh, magnanimous in defeat, charging into the England dressing room to celebrate, with huge ice packs on each knee to soothe the agony of bending down all day; of Brearley revealing gamesmanship by loudly discussing the weaknesses of an opposition batsman newly arrived at the crease.

The best portrait, however, is of Botham, Guy the Gorilla, whose phenomenal energy constantly manifests itself in endless practical jokes. No cricket bag is safe.

'I was reading the *Sun* in the dressing room the other day,' said Gower, 'when it suddenly burst into flames – not ignited by lust, but by Botham setting fire to it.'

In the field, Botham never leaves Gower alone, leaning on him, prodding him, teasing him like some vile child plaguing the life out of – once again – the endlessly good-natured labrador. If it came to the crunch, could the labrador control the vile child?

Talking to Gower, you become aware, too, of the alarming increase in Citadel Cricket, namely the growing isolation of the England team. Highly paid, hero-worshipped, paranoid because they may get dropped at any minute with a dramatic loss of income, constantly sniped at by the media, who regard every innings as a first night, the players have retreated into a tight little band, bitterly united against the encroaching outside world, particularly the selectors, the cricket commentators and the press.

As Gower points out: 'If you're shot at every time you go on to the field, you naturally draw closer to your colleagues. Even Brearley isn't one of us any more. Once you leave the cocoon of the England side, you miss out on the vital opinions of the dressing room.' This alienation is not helped by the sullen gracelessness of Willis, nor the boorishness of Botham.

Gower as captain could give England back a much-needed image of cheerfulness and good manners. He has the diplomacy to bridge the growing gap between England and her critics. Fortunately, too, he has youth on his side. One returns to the Pears Soap image. David Gower is preparing to be a beautiful captain.

Princess Michael of Kent

The Princess and I had been friends for some years. The following piece, when it appeared in October 1986, was heavily cut by the Mail on Sunday, *who also changed the phrase 'occasionally she can be manipulative', to 'she can be very manipulative', and headlined the piece 'The Pushy Princess'. As a result, the Princess sent me thirty pieces of silver. Many people, however, accused me of flattering her to the point of sycophancy.*

In 1979, shortly after her marriage, the new Princess Michael of Kent swept imperiously into a London bookshop and demanded a complete set of reference books.

'What kind of reference books?' stammered the assistant, somewhat taken aback.

'The lot,' said the Princess.

With characteristic gusto and Prussian efficiency, Princess Michael had embarked on a new career as an author.

Her book, due out on 9 October, will cause something of a sensation. Not only is it history at its most racily readable, but also reveals a great deal about the fascinating Princess herself and her tempestuous relationship with the Royal Family.

Recently I visited her at Kensington Palace, where she lives in a four-storey apartment with Prince Michael and their two children. Kensington Dallas, as it should be called, is a royal soap opera house – England's answer to South Fork – which houses, in other apartments, the Prince and Princess of Wales, Princess Margaret, Princess Alice, and the Duke and Duchess of Gloucester. And if the inhabitants don't actually glower over the communal breakfast table like J.R. and Clayton Farlow, *froideurs* constantly develop because some princeling's yells keep

81

Princess Margaret awake, or one of Princess Michael's cats uses Prince Charles's bay tree tubs as an earthbox.

Pink roses, falling over an ancient wall, clashed with red and black lampposts topped with gold crowns. From open windows on all sides came the escalating yelp of different royal drinks parties. Princess Michael and I sat in her exquisite pastel rose-scented garden, drinking iced tea flavoured with cinnamon as her cats peered out of the lush green foliage like a Rousseau painting. Waving towards the ancient wall, Princess Michael announced that the Wales (as she airily calls Charles and Diana) lived next door.

'Gimme a periscope,' I muttered, expecting that at any minute Prince Harry's football would fly over and scatter the perfection of the Iceberg roses. Did the Princess lob slugs that threatened her hostas back over the wall when no one was looking? No she said reprovingly, she did not.

Five foot eleven, with strong Slav features, huge slanting sage-green eyes and thick streaked blond hair curling to her shoulders like Charles I, she is one of the most beautiful woman one will ever see. Perhaps to combat an over-Cavalier image, she was wearing a blue and white silk dress with a big white Puritan collar.

What had prompted her to write a book?

'I used to be a very successful interior designer, but once I married Prince Michael I couldn't be at the beck and call of clients ringing in the middle of the night about leaking roofs. Then I had to sue a client for payment, there was an awkwardness. I needed a project other than working for charity. What was there left for a mad princess to do decently? History seemed a safe subject.'

Sapphire and diamond rings caught the setting sun as she talked; the voice – husky, smoky, siren-soft – reminds one of Dietrich.

'So I decided to write about eight famous ladies, including Catherine the Great and Marie Antoinette, who married kings and emperors in other countries, and how they influenced and were treated by the countries they moved to. I also wanted to include the bits history books leave out: that Maria Carolina, for example, was married to a glove fetishist. She had only to caress her long gloved arms to bring her boorish husband, King

Ferdinand, to heel; and that despite professing not to fancy him (he kept his boots on in bed), she bore him seventeen children. That's an awful lot of hugger mugger,' the Princess added wickedly.

'I was also fascinated that Catherine the Great used a lady-in-waiting as a tester to try out possible new lovers, and had them medically checked as well. You can't go round having one-night stands if you're an empress.'

How would the Royal Family react to such salacious revelations?

'The Queen', said Princess Michael warmly, 'has been endlessly supportive and given me access to the archives at Windsor. The Wales have been kind. But there will be jealousy from others,' she added broodily.

Princess Michael, or Marie Christine, as she is known, has never really fitted into the English royal mould, which prefers understatement and gifted amateurism to a somewhat yuppy professionalism. She is too smart, too witty, too dazzlingly theatrical and, towering as she does over the rest of the Royal Family, too tall.

From the start, she seemed to revel too much in public engagements, and the public, even worse, reciprocated this enjoyment. When she turned on the Christmas lights in Stroud, near her Gloucestershire house, she was so radiant, according to a bemused local official, she lit up the whole town before she'd touched a single switch.

Marie Christine's most difficult problem, however, is that because her husband, Prince Michael, is only a cousin of the Queen and a younger son to boot, he does not receive any salary from the Royal Purse. This seems very unfair when his elder brother, the Duke of Kent, gets £132,000 a year from the Queen, his sister Alexandra £125,800, and young Prince Andrew, on his marriage to Fergie, received a rise from £20,000 a year to £50,000.

Princess Michael is therefore in a Catch 22 situation. To make ends meet, she has continually to hustle for money; advising art galleries, seeking directorships for her husband, and now, she hopes, writing a best-selling book. The tragedy is that such hustling is frowned on as pushiness and commercialism by other members of the Royal Family, who are

83

shored up by a fat salary from the Queen.

Princess's Michael's other great problem was that because Prince Michael's parents were both dead, she had no in-laws to give her a helping hand. As a result there were gaffes. For her fortieth birthday, in 1985, for example, she was photographed stunningly in a strapless dress, her blond hair cascading over flawless shoulders. The more unscrupulous papers cropped the dress, so it appeared she was wearing nothing at all. Princesses do not strip. Royalty was not amused.

Staying at Windsor one Christmas where every one of the two hundred odd guests was falling over backwards to assure the Queen they were having a good time, she ruffled feathers by grumbling that her children's nanny had only a black and white television in her room. Worst of all, she got across her neighbour, Princess Margaret, not least perhaps because the press kept pointing out that Marie Christine was fulfilling public engagements more frequently and more gracefully.

Then in April 1985 real scandal struck, when a newspaper cruelly revealed that her father (whom Marie Christine hero-worshipped and always believed had spent the war in a concentration camp for defying the Nazis) had been a member of the SS, possibly the perpetrator of appalling atrocities. Amid the ensuing storm of publicity, Marie Christine braved Badminton Horse Trials the following weekend, where she was mobbed by the crowds. Standing beside her, I experienced at second hand the horror of being devoured by thousands of eyes and camera lenses avid for signs of distress. There were none. She was magnificent.

Later in 1985 it came out that her father had only been a token member of the SS ('Rather like being in the guards,' said one English peeress) and had done nothing discreditable. Public sympathy had swung right behind her, when suddenly another newspaper claimed that, disguising herself in a red wig, the Princess had been seeing a Texas oil millionaire. There is a tradition that royalty do not sue. With her back to the wall, the true professional, Princess Michael retired to her house in the country and finished her book.

Despite the fact that her crack lawyer, Sir David Napley, whom the Princess calls her 'tame barracuda' had advised her to deny that she identifies with any of the eight royal ladies she has written about, anyone reading the book will find understandable hurt and self-justification on almost every page.

The Princess herself has admitted that before every public appearance she prays: 'Please God, let me not make a gaffe.'

But, writes Princess Michael, 'While Marie Antoinette's virtues frequently went unnoticed, every mistake – either political or personal – was seized on by her enemies . . . she was the victim of a vicious and shrewdly sustained process of character assassination . . . all her life criticism surrounded her.'

Again, Princess Michael could be describing herself and her own relationship with the Royal Family and the press when she writes about Queen Victoria's daughter Vicky, who married a Prussian prince: 'She was vivacious, attractive and spontaneous, impulsive, generous, easy to hurt and envied by many. Nor was tact her strongest quality, though she later learnt from experience to bite her tongue . . . No matter how hard she tried . . . she clashed with Fritz's family. Tittle-tattle about her spread.'

In her perfumed garden, the Princess poured more iced tea, steered a wasp away from one of her cats, and denied rather too forcefully that she'd ever had herself in mind when she wrote the book: 'These eight women were real princesses, first ladies of their countries. They were the icing on the cake of political treaties, and when the treaties turned sour, the countries they'd moved to turned against the queens.'

In her introduction, Princess Michael has stated somewhat rashly that of all her eight ladies, Catherine the Great is the one she resembles most. So one swoops on the chapter that describes Catherine as a shrewd, calculating perfectionist, always short of money, who couldn't go a day without love, who was adored by her servants (her valet set fire to his house to distract the court from the fact that Catherine was giving birth to a lover's child) and that when she died – 'beneath the grandeur and triumphs of the Empress lay the insecurity of a provincial German Princess'.

Did Marie Christine get up at five every morning like Catherine? I asked cautiously.

'No,' the green eyes glinted. 'But nor, like Catherine, was I still a virgin seven years after I was married.'

How was she most like Catherine then?

She held up one of her cats to her face, their unblinking witchy stares unnervingly similar: 'That you will have to work out for yourself.'

Changing the subject firmly, she said she originally called the book: *Queens from a Far Country*. 'But the American publishers took me aside and said everyone will think you're writing a book about faggots.' Her husband, Prince Michael, she said, had thought up the new title: *Crowned in a Far Country*. He had also corrected her spelling and punctuation and taken out the more outrageous bits, which she had promptly put back in again.

She is lucky in having the nicest, most attractive of husbands. Immensely kind, utterly honourable, zanily funny and slightly eccentric, he turned up at a Gloucestershire party this winter in a floor-length Barbour and a child's white sunhat.

'Marriage,' said Princess Michael, rising briskly to dead-head a yellow rose, 'is finding someone you can share a flat with.'

But a husband who absolutely adores her must be a constant source of strength. His quietness douses her fire and tempers her recklessness. But if she sometimes snaps at him, using him as her cat's scratching board, she delightedly recounts when he gets the better of her.

'Some booksellers were coming for drinks,' she explained, 'and a lady's heel had gone through my precious eighteenth-century carpet. Sewing it up, I pricked my finger and must have caught bubonic plague from some long gone Arab. In the middle of the night, I woke with a red-hot golf ball under my arm – blood poisoning!'

Having kept her husband up for most of the rest of the night with her complaining, the Princess roused him at six. Was it too early to ring the doctor?

'Much too early,' he murmured sleepily, 'I think you are about to go back to sleep for a hundred years – thank God.'

How does she cope with two young children, two houses (doing most of the cooking herself), several jobs, endless engagements and trips abroad?

'Like Catherine, I am highly organised, and a chronic list-maker.'

She denies she is ferociously competitive: 'The only thing I seek is my own approval.'

But seeing her playing tennis in the country in a strange calf-length dress, her long hair streaming like a Valkyrie's from a sweat-band, matching the handsome Marquis of Reading (a local champion) stroke for stroke, it is hard to believe she doesn't want to win every point.

She can occasionally be manipulative. 'She'll ring you up, knowing you've got a helicopter, to ask if you know anyone who's got a helicopter,' grumbled one peer. But she is also gloriously, imaginatively generous. A bowl of just-picked mulberries will suddenly arrive on a warm summer afternoon. Two Christmases ago, she found out what my two dogs were called, and sent me scarlet towelling drying bags, beautifully embroidered with their names.

'My desire', she said, 'is to improve the quality of my life and those that touch mine.' This would sound pompous and bogus from anyone else, but she is in fact an inspired hostess.

Aristocrats, artists, writers, politicians are asked to her houses only because of their entertainment value. The sofas and chairs are arranged so that little groups can carry on intimate conversations in every language under the sun.

Any one evening, you may sit next to Tom Stoppard, Arianna Stassinopoulos, David Frost, an Italian prince or one of the more glamorous American senators. Ritzy English friends include the impossibly handsome Duke of Beaufort, with his anorexic figure and arctic blue eyes, and the dashing, thrice-married Earl of Suffolk and Berkshire, who had such a spectacular fiftieth birthday party recently, that for miles around the helicopters could be seen landing like swarms of fireflies.

Another close friend is the delectable Rosie, Lady Northampton, who, having sat down in a restaurant the other day, was enchanted to receive a bottle of Krug from a table of complete strangers who'd decided she had the most beautiful bottom in the room.

Mrs Thatcher is also a frequent guest.

'I'm mad about her,' said the Princess. 'She doesn't waffle or witter. She is a strong, powerful woman of great character, who knows what she wants and sets out to do it. When you have her to dinner you have the woman not the Prime Minister. Last time we met, Mrs Thatcher asked me when my book was coming out. I said I'd send her a copy. "No, No", she insisted. "I shall go into Hatchards and demand it in a loud voice. That will have more effect!" '

An American senator and his wife were due for dinner at any minute. Marie Christine wandered round picking roses for the table, her cat familiars trailing her with strange unearthly cries.

Wasn't she delighted she'd written such an entertaining book?

'My problem', she sighed, 'is that I'm never satisfied. I always notice another layer of perfection to be achieved.' She pointed to the Iceberg roses luminous in the dusk, spilling voluptuously over their neat lavender hedge. 'I don't think: how beautiful. I merely wonder what I've been feeding them that makes them grow too tall.'

The charming Watteau effect of the beautiful Princess gathering pale roses in a basket was spoilt by a relentless water-pump sound. Not content with desecrating Prince Charles's bay-tree tubs, Holly the cat was throwing up yellow froth flecked with grass on the flagstones.

The Princess took me on a quick whisk through the house, which, like the garden, is impeccably decorated in pale greys, whites, pastel pinks and yellows, except for the drawing room which is a marvellous contrast of corals and terracottas, with walls lined with books and tapestries.

'There is not a light switch in this place that is not designed by me,' said the Princess.

From a top-floor room, I caught a glimpse of the Wales's garden, its blaze of flowers positively gaudy compared with the pastel perfection of Princess Michael's patch. Did her children, Lord Frederick (seven) and Lady Gabriella (five), get on with Prince William and Prince Harry?

'Oh yes, our two front doors are always open, children keep running in for a biscuit or a cat. Ella and William are great friends.'

Enchanting Ella, with one eye half green, half gold, like her grandmother Princess Marina, was waiting for her mother to read her a bedtime story.

'I like naughty stories best,' she announced.

One so hopes the public agree and buy thousands of copies of her mother's book, so that the 'insecure provincial Princess' gets the recognition and financial reward she so longs for. For above all Marie Christine is a life-enhancer.

Recently a man came to mend my washing-machine. The trouble, he explained, had been caused by dog biscuits in the filter. He then went on to boast that that morning he'd mended Princess Michael's washing machine.

'What was wrong with hers?' I asked.

'She had three gold sovereigns in her filter,' he said.

East Enders

Part One

EastEnders is a phenomenon. Twice a week, an incredible twenty-one million viewers of all ages and classes tune in to the goings-on in Albert Square. In playground and common room alike, speculation is endless. Will Michelle lose her baby? Will Dirty Den, the Queen Vic's shifty landlord, leave his tarty wife for his dowdy mistress?

This month, *EastEnders* celebrates its first birthday. Being an avid fan, I visited the BBC studios at Boreham Wood where the supersoap is being made.

To my excitement, the first person I saw was Leslie Grantham who plays Dirty Den. Wearing a peacock blue shirt, he was prowling through a crowd of schoolgirls. I was staggered that they totally ignored the nation's number one heart-throb until I realised they were the cast of *Grange Hill* going for their elevenses.

Up in the press office, the telephones rang constantly. Judy Curren, the assistant press officer, serene in a dark blue jersey, needs the skill of a Peter Shilton to deflect a press ravening for scandal about the cast. The *Sun* has been ordered to have an *EastEnders* story in the paper every day.

My heart sank when Judy told me that for this reason Leslie Grantham was not prepared to be interviewed. He felt he had been over-exposed recently.

At that moment, Roly the Queen Vic's poodle, still with his orange baby fur, trotted in looking for company. He was missing his friend, Willy the pug, who was not on the set today.

Both dogs, said Judy, got a vast fan mail, and would have

90

made a fortune in stud fees, but sadly they'd been neutered – presumably to stop the *Sun* writing about their sex lives.

To make up for not meeting Dirty Den, I was taken to see Peter Dean. He plays Pete Beale, Dirty Den's best mate, a caring goody who mans a fruit and veg stall in Albert Square and wears a hideous tweed hat like an inverted flower pot.

In the flesh he is very attractive, dark blond, with denim blue eyes, a boxer's flattened nose and hunky body, long muscular legs, and bare feet, because Wardrobe had lost his socks. The schedule for *EastEnders*, he admits, is punishing. The actors work six days a week, rehearsing Monday, Tuesday and Saturday, recording inside from 10 a.m. to 10 p.m. on Wednesday and Thursday, and filming exterior shots in Albert Square on Friday. Sunday, the one day off, is devoted to learning lines.

Working so flat out, it's not surprising the cast look authentically drawn and disadvantaged.

'Rudolph Hess has 'ad more free time than me in the past year,' said Pete cheerfully. 'But it's the 'appiest company; been that way from the beginning'.

A cockney like most of the cast, Pete and his family have always worked in street markets.

'My Mum's very proud of my acting career,' he confessed. 'But she does get muddled. I once acted in a play at the King's Head pub, in Islington. A week later, I rang Mum up and told her I'd got a part in Shakespeare. "Ow", she said, "is that the pub in the Mile End Road?" When she heard I'd landed a part in *EastEnders*, the phone just went dead. The whole street knew in twenty-five seconds.'

Before *EastEnders*, Pete always played villains. As Pete Beale, he was relieved to play a good guy for a change, but soon realised how hard it was.

'I'm the Bobby Ewing of Albert Square. Cath and I are Mr and Mrs Nice Guy, which can so easily become Mr and Mrs Boring.'

To the uninitiated, in the story, Cath, Pete's wife, was raped and had a baby at fourteen, which she was too ashamed to tell Pete about, even when the dastardly Nick Cotton, the Iago of Albert Square, started blackmailing her. One of the most moving scenes was when she finally screwed up her courage to

91

tell Pete the truth.

'The extraordinary thing', said Pete, 'is that so many of the public think we're real. Hundreds of people wrote in, warning me that Cath was being blackmailed.'

EastEnders also has an enormous appeal to children, perhaps because it shows parents in a realistic light.

'I was mobbed at a gymkhana last summer,' explained Pete. 'All the kids crowded round saying: "We love you and Cath, you're just like our Mums and Dads." I was really pleased and said: "In what way?" They said: "You're always acting silly between yourselves, drinking and quarrelling, and you only speak to us to tell us off or when you want us to do something." '

Nor is it just the public who confuse the actors and the roles they play'.

'My accountant gave me a form to fill in the other day,' said Pete. 'I found I'd put down my address as Albert Square.' In real life, he and his wife live in Finchley, near Mrs Thatcher: 'Now there's a lady I would really love to shake by the neck.'

EastEnders like most acting jobs requires lots of hanging around: 'I've been here since ten o'clock and I've only 'ad one line, and I effed that up by calling Cath, Gilly.'

Peter obviously has great affection and admiration for his co-star, Gilly Taylforth, who plays the sullen, somewhat taciturn Cath. Imagining her like her stage character, I was wary of meeting her, but she turned out as bubbly as Goldie Hawn, sentences spilling out like coins from the jackpot. She is also much prettier off the screen, with a peachy skin, slanting eyes, soft flopping aconite-yellow hair and a gold bracelet on one slender ankle.

Cards, mostly Beryl Cook fat ladies, celebrating her thirtieth birthday were sellotaped to her dressing-room walls. She was reading a note saying: 'Gilly, can you please sign this poster for a man named Grisly.'

Thrilled by the success of *EastEnders*, she finds the adulation bewildering: 'I can't get used to people staring at me in the street, I keep thinking my slip's showing. And I've suddenly become other people's property, women grab me at functions and tell me to kiss their 'usbands. It's only because I'm a cockney; they wouldn't do it to Penny Keith.'

92

She has perhaps remained so unspoilt by success because her staunch, undemonstrative family keep her feet on the ground.

'My Dad never says anything about the programme except occasionally: ''You was fair.'' But after the scene when I had to tell Pete about the rape, he rang me at my flat. ''I didn't know we had a Bette Davis in the family,'' he said, ''thought you was marvellous.'' I was so choked I could only say, ''Where's Mum?'' Dad said: ''She's out.'' He couldn't have told me I was good in front of her.'

How did she find time to keep her flat clean?

'With great difficulty. I 'ave a polish on Sundays. My idea of a great night out is taking four bags of washing down to the launderette.'

Back in Peter Dean's dressing room, I found Nick Berry, who plays Pete's son, Wicksy.

'I'm on the set in a minute,' he said, going towards the basin. 'Got to clean my teeth.'

'I clean mine fourteen times a day till my gums bleed,' said Pete. 'Actors are obsessed with bad breaff, terrified of offending someone. Except for Joan Collins, who so 'ated one of her co-stars, she always chewed garlic before their love scenes.'

We were joined by Ethel, the Queen Vic's erratic charlady, played by Gretchen Franklyn. A cross between the White Queen, and the wily old heroine of *The Lady Killers*, she has the innocent eyes of a kitten, a gentle smile, and a drawling voice. She was wearing one roller in her fringe, a tweed skirt, a gardening cardigan, purple snow boots and a blue and white beach skirt.

She was so sad I wasn't going to meet Willy the pug, she said, as though this was an experience no serious person should miss.

How had her life changed since *EastEnders*?

'Not for the better,' she said darkly. 'I haven't got time to go to the dentist, the doctor, the optician nor the corn plasterer. I had offered my body to medical research, but now they'll refuse it.'

She turned to Pete and Wicksy, who was cleaning his teeth again.

I'm going to wear a most interesting hat this afternoon. A viewer left it behind in my house. People send lovely presents to Willy you know: dog chews, a set of golf balls, lots of photos of pugs. He came on Wogan with me. Wogan is a charming man, but he wouldn't kiss Willy.'

She shook her head incredulously and wandered off.

Wicksy, exuding Colegate and handsome amiability, flashed his flawless teeth and admitted he got a huge fan mail from teenage girls. It made him feel rotten sometimes. One school girl had asked him to meet her outside her school gates in her lunch hour today. 'She'll be so choked when I don't turn up.'

'Women write asking me to bring my cucumbers round to their flat,' said Pete. 'But if I go to a charity do, I leave by ten. Boyfriends who've had a few too many get nasty and suddenly come up saying: "My girlfriend fancies you." You may think you're got a private life, but you 'aven't anymore.'

Like a small boy putting on a policeman's helmet to make the grown-ups laugh, Ethel returned to show off her interesting hat, a massive brown fur bonnet with pompoms. We all giggled. She looked delighted.

'You'd be better off with a husky than a pug in that' teased Wicksy.

'Willy was a poodle when the series began,' said Pete. 'It's only you shoving the pub door open with his nose so often that's turned him into a pug.'

Like a kindly sheepdog, Wicksy guided Ethel off to do her next scene.

Down in the vast studio, wires hung down everywhere like lianas. Like rooms of a giant doll's house, or a very un-Ideal Home exhibition waiting to be assembled, stand the interior sets of Albert Square. There was the Fowlers' sitting room, with its dingy wallpaper, scruffy furniture and pictures that would make the Green Park Railing School look like the Tate.

Julia Smith, the producer, is a perfectionist. In Aly's café all the ovens work. The menu on the blackboard – today it was toad-in-the-hole, mash and peas – is written in by the same actor every day to give continuity. All the machines in the launderette work, and the pub is masterly, the perfect reconstruction of a Victorian pub. They even have their own Luxford and Copley beer mats printed.

And *there* was the telephone on which Dirty Den makes all his fiddles and rings his mistress. If that worked, maybe I could interview that instead.

94

In the scene being shot, Andy the Scots male nurse, very handsome and radiating dependability, was telling Mary the Punk that she was a nice wee girl beneath all that make-up. Mary's baby disagreed and was bawling lustily on the bed.

'When the baby cries we usually let it cry on,' said one of the Associate Producers. 'It makes the scene more realistic.'

'You're a nice wee girl,' bellowed Andy.

The baby bawled even louder.

'Let's do this scene without the baby,' said the director.

Now it was a pub scene, and Ethel's turn to cry over some drama with Willy. Dirty Den lounged in the doorway wearing a dark suit and a blue striped tie. Pale, cadaverous, like a sexy undertaker, he has an alsatian quality about him, something unpredictable, untamed: one would not take liberties. I had to admit he was wonderfully well constructed, but also noticed he has a bald patch shaped like a diamond.

'He gets far the most fan mail,' whispered the Associate Producer reverently. Perhaps they should rename the programme *Denasty*.

Upstairs in a glass box, Keith Harris, the senior designer, watched every scene on a monitor with the sound turned down.

'I'm not interested in what they say, only what it looks like,' he said. 'I have to watch all the time in case a cameraman leaves a script on the bar. When I get out of here at ten o'clock at night, I feel like a pit pony.'

Beside him were several aerosol cans. Hairspray for aging up furniture. Anti-Flare, which sounds like something teenagers squirt on their parents' trousers, to spray on food containers on the bar, so they don't reflect the lights too much.

In the control room, the appropriately named vision mixer, a beautiful redhead, gazed at all the different monitors, pressing coloured buttons to change the picture. Next door to her the director, Michael Lloyd, gave advice to the actors on the floor, while listening to instructions from Julia Smith in the producer's box.

Back in the press office, I found Nejdet Salih, the Cypriot who plays Aly, the Cypriot café owner. Known because of his sex appeal as Aly the Stallion, he looks, with his dark collarbone-length hair, big hooked nose and soulful tarmac-black eyes, more like a stocky little ram. He was wearing a black shirt, and lots of jewellery. He has great charm.

'I love *EastEnders*,' he said. 'I live it, smell it, breathe it.' It was in fact his first big acting break. 'My father wanted me to be a lawyer or a doctor, and insisted I went into an office. He'd even arranged a marriage for me, but she was an ugly cow – although she might not be now,' he added hastily. 'So the moment my father died, I broke it off, and started going to drama classes in the evening. It's difficult becoming an actor if you're working class. All your mates think you've turned gay.'

His hands move as he talks, amethysts and gold rings flashing in the neon light.

'Originally, they was looking for a Greek to play Aly. I turned up at the audition, I didn't know whether to put on a posh accent. We was all so brainwashed at drama school to talk like Jeremy Irons. But I decided for once to go back to my cockney roots. Sandy Radcliffe, who plays my wife Sue in *EastEnders*, was late, so I turned to her and snapped: "Typical of a woman, keeping a man waiting, don't do it again." Everyone looked amazed, and said: "Has someone told you the story line?" So I played the part all macho.'

'Three days later, I got a letter from the BBC. It was so complicated, I couldn't work out if I'd got the job. I rang my agent and said: "I may have some good news for you." '

Nej (it rhymes with Reg) is amazed he gets so much adulation from women. I always thought successful actors was tall and handsome. I'm only five foot five, but they write to me telling me I'm gorgeous and a hunk, and come and stroke my hair in the street. Shopping's a bit difficult,' he sighed. 'They peer into the freezer at the supermarket, and yell: "Let's see what he's 'aving for his tea." You feel guilty if it's smoked salmon.'

What about his alleged romance with Linda Davidson, who plays Mary the Punk. Nej's eyes flickered. He said he'd rather not talk about it.

Linda Davidson, sitting in her dressing room surrounded by cards from Nej saying he loves her, Get Well cards from Nej, and photographs of Nej, had no such reservations.

'He's the first boyfriend my mother's liked,' she said. 'And tonight,' she blushed under her chalk-white punk make-up, 'he's cooking me supper.'

'Smoked salmon?'

96

'No – cod in cheese sauce – out of a packet,' she added dreamily. 'Nej has got such charisma.'

Out in the passage, a large lady swept past, shouting to a group of *Grange Hill* boys to collect their blazers from upstairs. Her exhortations fell on deaf ears. The boys were gazing longingly at Letitia Dean (who plays Dirty Den's wayward daughter), who was teetering past on four-inch heels, a pink fluffy sweater emphasising her forty-two-inch bust.

6.45 p.m.: It seemed like midnight. On the set – another pub scene. Sharon and Den's wife Angie (her over-made-up face twitching with emotion) were having a row. In front of the photograph of Charles and Diana, Wicksy was flashing his teeth like Liberace's grandson. An extra was removed for cluttering up the scene. Wicksy happily obeyed orders to move closer to Cath. Den in the hall was gazing gloomily at the wallpaper – well he might – it was hideous.

As Sharon flounced past, he grabbed her arm.

'We've gotta talk, Princess.'

Idly I wondered if Prince Charles ever says that to Diana.

Back in Pete's dressing room, Wicksy cleaned his teeth again. Pete was talking to June Brown, the marvellous actress who plays Dot Cotton. A kind of Discount Dracula, she has a sardonic vampire's face, an iron filings voice and thin scarlet lips which draw on endless cigarettes. All the cast bring her their problems, as she really listens.

As the mother of the fiendish Nick Cotton, who has left the show temporarily to appear in pantomime, she got lots of sympathetic letters. Her favourite came from a five-year-old.

'Dear Dot, I'm writing to tell you, your son Nick is in Newcastle in a play. He isn't bad anymore and didn't mean to steal your earrings, so don't worry Dot. P.S. Can my sister have a picture of Wicksy?'

By the coffee machine Maul and Lil, two *EastEnders* stallholders with peroxide hair and knowing faces, were tarting up for a night scene in the Queen Vic. Both wore turquoise cashmere jerseys – 'must 'ave come off the back of a lorry' – and more *diamanté* swag than Barbara Cartland.

All the cast were lovely people, they said. It was a great team. Although, Lil added, she always brought her own knife, fork, plate and plastic champagne glass in with her because she was so terrified of catching Aids.

It was 9 p.m. In the passage, I bumped into Dirty Den. He looked shattered, his eyes black hollows in a putty-coloured face. I begged him to talk to me – just for a few minutes.

'It's been a sod of a day,' he said. 'I've been on the set since ten this morning. Anyway I'm terrified you'll find out how boring I am,' and slid like a fox back on to the set.

Linda Davidson (prettily pink-cheeked and red-gold-haired now that her punk make-up and hair dye had been washed out) and Gilly Taylforth were going home. They said how much they liked today's director. 'He was calm and didn't interfere.' Outside the control room, a technician, just off duty, said he was going to send the director a wallygram. 'I mean he is supposed to direct,' he added petulantly.

'The actors like him.'

'Actors don't know anything. If an actor asks me: what is my motivation in this scene? I tell him: pay day on Thursday.'

9.55 p.m.: Angie was chucking eggs into a frying pan for Sharon's breakfast, but they didn't fry quickly enough. Time was up. Even if they'd been acting like Trevor Howard and Celia Johnson, the scene would be scrapped and started again in the morning.

Thank you all very much,' said the director. 'It's been a long day, and I do appreciate it.'

In reception, the taxi drivers waited for the stars. Julia Smith, the producer, came past preceded by Roly the poodle, bouncy in anticipation of a late-night walk. Leslie Grantham was on the telephone talking in a lowered voice. My mini cab hadn't arrived and as all the cast left, they bid me a jolly good night, and asked if I was OK for a lift.

The director, who was staying at a hotel nearby, even offered to drive me into London. Finally at 10.35, when the mini cab still hadn't arrived, Leslie Grantham came off the telephone.

'Would you like a lift into London?' he said softly.

To my eternal shame, some middle-class inhibition, some crippling shyness, some wish not to bother him, all overwhelmed me. I stammered I was fine. All over England, I could hear ten million besotted female fans muttering: you
98

blithering idiot.

It was no comfort when I finally got back to the Garrick Club to hear a judge confidently assuring two barristers over a midnight brandy that Dirty Den was definitely turning gay.

Part Two

Wandering, on my second visit to *EastEnders*, through the beautifully kept BBC garden with its manicured shrubs and frozen fish ponds, it was a shock to find myself suddenly in the slums. For the Albert Square set built for *EastEnders* is so stunningly realistic you can't believe you're not in the most derelict part of the East End, or, even more incredibly, that houses are just shells made of plywood and fibreglass.

Dominating the square is Dirty Den's pub, the Queen Vic, with its tatty peeling paint and rusty hanging baskets swinging in the icy wind. The pavement outside must be the coldest spot in the world, the sort of place Eskimos send their children as punishment.

When I finally managed to interview Leslie Grantham, back in the press office, the welcome was equally chilly. He seems to put up defensive barriers, because he is terrified that people will discover that – like his pub in Albert Square – his handsome, slightly battered exterior is nothing but a shell and an illusion.

To understand both Leslie's paranoia and the magnitude of his achievement, we have to go back to 1966, when at the age of just eighteen he was jailed for life, accused of murdering and robbing a taxi driver while he was in the army in Germany.

He did eleven years, but towards the end of his sentence was allowed out to go to interviews at drama schools.

'Can't have been easy,' said one of the *EastEnders* cast, 'declaiming "To Be Or Not To Be" with handcuffs on.'

But Leslie was accepted by the Webber Douglas Drama School and set about rebuilding his life. After several minor parts including appearances in *Dr Who* and *The Jewel In The Crown*, he landed the star role in *EastEnders*. Immediately he had the guts and sense to level with Julia Smith, the programme's despotic but understanding producer.

'He told me all about his past,' said Julia, 'which was an incredibly brave things to do. I said, "Let's be positive, let's face it if and when it comes out." Leslie simply couldn't believe

99

I was going to keep him on.'

Immediately the programme went out on the air, the press put two and two together and the storm broke. The BBC, however, stood firm and the ratings soared, with Leslie, the prodigal son, emerging as a star attraction. Everyone was for Dirty Dennis.

Like the rescued dog, who, after being badly treated in early life, is taken into a loving home, Leslie's loyalty to his new master *EastEnders* is unassailable and deeply protective. Again as I talked to him, he reminded me of the rescued alsatian. He has the same long face, the watchful acorn-brown eyes, the wolf-like grace, the unpredictability and the aggression hiding the intense vulnerability. Appropriately dressed in a thundercloud-grey sweater and trousers, he was very pale, the black hair falling in tendrils over his forehead, his mouth set in a thin line. Determined not to betray any emotion he is, however, highly intelligent and, when he relaxes, marvellously irreverent.

At drama school, according to a fellow student, Leslie had to overcome chips both about being working-class cockney and about his past. Having been inside at an age when he should have been wowing the girls, it took him a long time to appreciate how attractive he was. He over-compensated at first by pulling nearly everything in sight. But if a pretty girl talked to him he still worried that she was winding him up.

On a first date, he stood up drama student Jane Laurie because he couldn't believe that a beautiful middle-class girl with a rich father could really fancy him. In the end she did the proposing – and they've been happily married for five years.

'Any children?' I asked.

He half grinned:'No, we're still practising, but we'd like a baby soon.'

In fact both he and Jane have been too busy with their careers. Last year she played Pandora, the ravishingly pretty reporter in *Lytton's Diary*.

'What makes her really fed up,' said Leslie, 'is when journalists take her out to lunch to talk about her career and spend the time pumping her about me.'

They have a house in Fulham. 'People leave us alone there. The only problem is you come home shattered after a twelve-hour stint on *EastEnders* and you've just got to sleep when all the

Hooray Henrys wake you up yelling and banging their GTI doors at 3 a.m. And I tend to get fed up when journalists ring my doorbell in the middle of the night to ask whether I'm turning gay. I just say, "No – but my husband is," and slam the door in their faces.'

Although he's been known to get his clothes ripped off by women when he makes personal appearances, usually the alsatian quality keeps people at a distance.

'I can even travel on the Tube without people bothering me. They stare, and nudge each other and say: "D'you fink that's 'im? No it can't be, stars don't travel on the Tube." They don't realise no one's going to be a millionaire on a BBC salary.'

He's not doing too badly, however. He recently gave Jane a BMW and at Christmas took her away for a five-day break in a Cheshire hotel. The only drawback was leaving Russell, their black-and-white cat whom Leslie plainly adores.

'I was worried he'd get lonely. A mate told me if you left five bowls of cat food covered with Clingfilm the cat would break it with his paw each day when he got hungry. I spent bloody hours trying to teach Russell to break the Clingfilm. But he just purred and rolled over on his back' – a natural reaction of most women when confronted by Mr Grantham.

What did he feel about Roly, the Queen Vic poodle?

'As Dirty Den, I'm supposed to adore him. But we have a sort of love-hate relationship. He's such a stupid dog – he's like a *Sun* reporter, 'angs around all day but never does anything constructive.'

While not a versatile character actor like Olivier, or a classical juvenile lead, Leslie is brilliant, like Redford, at projecting his own personality on the screen.

A tinge of colour came into the pale face when I said how good he was.

'Well, I work very hard at the brush strokes. That's why I go on the Tube and make myself go out. An actor's got to study people. If you isolate yourself you've nothing to feed on.'

Like all the *EastEnders'* cast, he is addicted to old movies. His favourite actor is Robert Mitchum, another personality actor, whose deadpan style Leslie tries to emulate.

One suspects a touch of inverted snobbery and professional jealousy in his intense dislike of up-market heart-throbs like

Jeremy Irons, Anthony Andrews, Rupert Everett and even Jason Connery.

'They all come from the MFI furniture shop school of acting.'

'What's that?'

'Wooden.'

Wasn't that a case of the deadpan calling the pot black?

Like many insecure people, he can be bitchy and insensitive, particularly towards his own sex. The cast, who like and admire him, say he has moments of frantic name-dropping, even megalomania when he refers to *EastEnders* as 'My Show'.

And, on the flipside, moments of panic. When he read the script and found that, as well as having a mistress and an embattled wife, he was to emerge as the father of teenage Michelle's baby, he wanted the part changed. He was terrified the public would stop sympathising with the character.

'He can't realise', said Julia Smith, 'that the public really love him and that by his success he has given hope to thousands of people.'

The secret of sex appeal is more hard to define. Julia Smith believes it is the haunting, vulnerable quality that stems from what he has suffered. As the troubled, misunderstood loner, he is a direct descendant of James Dean and Frank Sinatra as Pal Joey. Watching him, women feel he's only behaving badly because he's unhappy and needs the love of a good woman. As Dirty Den he has the love of at least three.

Another reason the programme succeeds is that it not only makes the viewers laugh and cry, it also makes them wait. For nearly a year now, Dirty Den has had snatched conversations on the Queen Vic telephone with his mistress, Jan, without her making an appearance.

Just when we believed it would be always Jan tomorrow, never Jan today, she suddenly made a dramatic appearance in the pub three weeks ago. Hardly a soap dish, she turned out a most bizarre mixture – as though Shirley Williams had not only become a Sloane Ranger, but had also acquired Mrs Thatcher's slow-measured voice when she's being 'deeply caring' about some national disaster.

How did Leslie fancy his mistress now she'd finally arrived?

Again he grinned wickedly. 'Mates keep ringing up complaining she looks more like my mother.'

Jane How, who plays Jan, was more chivalrous when I rang her, describing Leslie in her intensely theatrical baritone voice as a 'wonderful, truly caring man'.

'Of course,' she went on, 'he's a leading man in all senses of the word. He pulls the whole cast.'

'Really,' I squeaked in excitement.

'Together,' she added firmly. 'If anyone's a bit down, Leslie jollies them along. Without him I think the whole programme might disintegrate into factions and sniping.'

Back to Leslie. Wasn't he gratified that he pulls in three times as much fan mail as anyone else?

He shrugged: 'There's more stars in this programme than the Planetarium. If the microphone gets in shot it gets fan mail.'

Before *EastEnders*, in between acting parts, Leslie took a job as a bingo caller, painted a VD clinic and worked in Piero di Monzi, a smart clothes shop in the Fulham Road where he served all the stars.

What were they like? He thought for a minute.

'Most people in this profession are so far up themselves, they wear themselves as a wig. Acting's about paying your mortgage. I get fed up with actors who keep asking: "Would this part be good for my career?" They never think if they'd be good for the poor audience. The only thing that matters in acting is whether Aunt Marjorie in Manchester wants to know if he's knocking her off or not. If you lose credibility, you lose your audience.'

A minion arrived to summon him back to the set.

'What we combine in *EastEnders*,' said Leslie, 'is a bloody good story with believable characters who explore problems that are usually only tackled on Channel 4 at 3.30 a.m. *EastEnders* works because it reaches the parts other soaps don't reach.'

This week *EastEnders* celebrates a triumphant first birthday. One can only wish the super soap many happy returns . . . and hope that for Leslie Grantham the bubble never bursts.

Lord Hailsham

This piece was written in May 1985, when there was some speculation that Lord Hailsham should be replaced as Lord Chancellor by a younger man. Happily he survived this minor storm and was only replaced after the Election in June 1987. Happily, since then he has has also remarried.

'Forgive me if I don't get up,' said Lord Hailsham. 'My leaping days are over.'   Not so Spotty, his Jack Russell puppy, who, totally unawed by his master's splendid office in the House of Lords, leapt all over the desk, scattering papers, bulldog clips and white quill pens.

'I am no good at training dogs,' said Lord Hailsham. 'My spaniel, Mr Jones, always sang with excitement when I took him shooting and never passed his O levels retrieving. Sit, Spotty.'

Spotty took no notice.

'Only Maggie can control him,' sighed the Lord Chancellor. 'A word from her, a steely look, and Spotty capitulates: he recognises the ultimate authority.'   Envisaging a thrilling new Barbara Woodhouse career for Mrs Thatcher, I said I didn't know she liked dogs.

'No, no, Maggie my driver. The PM is always Margaret.'

His eyes creased with laughter. He is a huge tease.

The round face, full of wisdom and kindness, has a beaky nose, pixie ears, and rather wild wrinkles on his forehead, as though the wind had blown them askew. Like a garden gnome rigged out for town, he wore striped trousers and a black coat, softened by a scarlet handkerchief and a scattering of dog hairs. Nearly seventy-eight, his mind is as needle-sharp as Spotty's teeth.

As Lord Chancellor heading a ten-thousand strong department, he runs the courts, appoints judges, and has instigated many reforms in civil law. As a senior minister, he also provides one of the few voices of distinction and scholarship in the cabinet. Mrs Thatcher not only finds his waspish humour invaluable for pricking the bubbles of her more pompous colleagues, but is also reassured by his wealth of experience.

He is unshocked, for example, by the increased thuggery in the House, Mr Kinnock calling Mrs T a twister, David Owen being howled down by Labour yobbos.

'Politics was far rougher before World War One. Feeling ran much higher. Asquith was repeatedly howled down, and I remember my uncle telling me how Ronnie Macneil, who later became Lord Cushendon, hurled Erskine May across the House.'

'Who was he?'

'He was a very large book,' said Lord Hailsham kindly.

The pedagogic precision is always tempered by dramatic pauses and great wheezes of laughter like a huge bellows.

Quintin Hailsham was born into an intensely political and legal family. His beautiful American mother was a judge's daughter. His brilliant lawyer father went straight on to the front bench, as Bonar Law's attorney general, became Lord Chancellor and was strongly tipped as a future leader.

Little Quintin's now famous qualities of unassailable loyalty and eruptive temper had established themselves by the age of two when his nanny was sacked for hitting him.

'I was devoted to Nanny, even if she did hit me. When my mother – whom I held entirely responsible for Nanny's departure – came to say goodnight afterwards, I quoted Beatrix Potter, with whose works I was already familiar, and shouted: "Go away you ugly old toad." '

At six he showed further evidence of independence.

'I had heard my father discussing the Irish Question, and announced in the nursery that I couldn't see why the Irish couldn't rule themselves. My half-brother sneaked to my father, who gravely chided me for being a very silly little boy. I have been a Conservative ever since.'

The cleverest boy ever to go to Eton, a double first at Oxford where he notched up more alphas than anyone since Gladstone,

105

he secured Oxford for the Tories in 1928, and made such an impressive maiden speech that MPs tipped him as a future Lord Chancellor.

All dreams of a political career where shattered when his father was offered a peerage.

'I begged him not to take it, correctly divining that the House of Lords would not be the way to the top. Unfortunately my stepmother, a country parson's daughter from Kenya, not the calibre of my mother, rather Memsahib in fact (again the bellows wheezes of laughter), was attracted to the peerage and persuaded my father to accept. Alas, a step up for her was a step down for me.'

As a future peer, realising he would be forced to play for the second eleven, he turned to his first love, the law. But, as with his contemporary at Eton, Randolph Churchill, this second brilliant career was halted by the war. Although he was repeatedly offered high-powered desk jobs, Lord Hailsham 'having voted for the war' was with characteristic integrity determined to fight in it. Joining the Rifle Brigade, he was wounded in the Western Desert.

In his lifetime, he has served under seven prime ministers. Chamberlain, he stresses, was much maligned.

'He saved the country at Munich. He knew if we'd gone to war in 1938, we'd have been hopelessly unprepared.'

Churchill, by contrast, was a genius brought in by providence. 'If Winston had not been in the wilderness until 1940, he'd have been hopelessly compromised by his earlier decisions. As it was, he got it as wrong as anyone. He told me France would hold out and mobilise millions, that Turkey would come in on our side. He was wildly over-optimistic.'

After the war, Lord Hailsham returned joyfully to the bar. But in 1955 – at a fraction of the salary he was earning as a lawyer – he somewhat reluctantly accepted the post of First Lord of the Admiralty in Anthony Eden's government. Immediately he was catapulted into the Suez crisis, where at the beginning Eden kept him very much in the dark.

'Ships were mobilising without my knowing anything about it, it was rather a shock.'

Later Lord Hailsham and his wife were giving a children's party at Admiralty House.

'Hoards of little ones sliding down the bannisters, when suddenly Eden summoned me. He sent for the Secretaries of State for War and Air as well. We all arrived with our trousers padded, bearing files to justify whatever misdemeanour we were supposed to have committed, only to be told Eden was resigning. He was not a prime minister – too much of a fusspot, too preoccupied with detail, and what other people's departments were doing.'

Lord Hailsham's great triumph, which he refers to in legal terms as 'my most important case (unpaid)', was as party chairman orchestrating the Tory landslide of one hundred seats in 1959, after Tory popularity had hit rock bottom two years before. With his bicycling to work, bell ringing, and bathing at party conferences, Lord Hailsham made himself so well known in the country that Macmillan became jealous and for a time relations were frosty between them.

'Harold Macmillan was on the devious side,' said Lord Hailsham broodingly. 'But at least he was unflappable.' He brightened. 'I invented that word. Macmillan had whizzed off to Australia, having described the resignation of Peter Thorneycroft, the Chancellor of the Exchequer, with more panache than judgement as "a little local difficulty". I was left to smooth things over. Refusing to suck up and describe Macmillan as a great leader, I described him as "unflappable". The word has now passed into the language.'

The refusal to suck up may have cost him the leadership. In 1963, when Macmillan resigned from ill-health after the Profumo crisis, Quintin Hailsham was his first choice as successor. Hailsham promptly announced his intention to renounce his peerage at the party conference.

'It was a jam-packed electric occasion,' remembers a Tory MP. 'Quintin came across as a brilliant, vibrant, wonderfully exciting orator, in direct line from Disraeli, Lloyd George, Churchill. By comparison, Butler and Maudling seemed drab and lifeless. When Quintin announced he was giving up his peerage, the cheering nearly blew the roof off.'

But tragically, things went wrong. Quintin Hogg, as he was now called again, was loved by the Tory rank and file but had enemies in the cabinet. To people who absorb the butter of flattery quicker than a frying aubergine, he was abrasive and

107

unpredictable.

'He always speaks his mind,' said an ex-minister. 'And although he apologises afterwards, it can be very disagreeable until he does. He could, and still can be, insensitive to atmosphere, banging on at cabinet meetings. You can sit back and enjoy the distraction, saying this is frightfully good stuff, but self-important, rather mediocre people think it's wasting time.'

He was perhaps too emotional, too volatile, a touch exhibitionist. The English love eccentrics, but prefer them caged in an Oxford quad, or writing poetry like John Betjemen. Macmillan, persuaded by the cabinet to play safe, chose the reticent, mild-mannered, diplomatic Lord Home, who waited to renounce his peerage until he had the leadership in the bag.

Today Lord Hailsham plays down his disappointment. 'Being prime minister doesn't bring happiness.'

But until then he had regularly written poetry. With the loss of the leadership, the muse deserted him too. He never wrote another line.

'In fact Quintin was heartbroken,' said a fellow MP and close friend. 'Bitterly disappointed. And it was a tragedy. He would have made a great prime minister, an intellectual giant, utterly fearless, with total integrity. People question his judgement, but on important matters he was always right: about wanting us to join Europe straight after the war, about the colour problem, denouncing Enoch Powell's rivers of blood speech and tempering much right-wing opinion.'

Did he think himself he would have made a great prime minister?

Lord Hailsham examined the thin, jeaned legs of a workman sidling along his window ledge, and then smiled.

'As the White Knight remarked, I do not say it would have been better. I only say it would have been different.'

True to form, he served with the utmost loyalty under Alec Douglas-Home ('the nicest prime minister there's ever been, but stronger on foreign policy than at home'), and later as Lord Chancellor under Edward Heath, whom he liked but found 'difficult to reach personally'.

Although he wept openly when Heath was ousted by Mrs Thatcher, always putting party before self, he instantly transferred his loyalty to the new leader, and was rewarded in 1979, when she gave him a second stint as Lord Chancellor.

As someone who considered party loyalty all-important, didn't he feel Heath had been rotten to Mrs Thatcher? Lord Hailsham shrugged: 'One must not underestimate how traumatic it was for Edward Heath to be ejected by Margaret Thatcher. To have just missed being prime minister as I did was bad enough. But as Chief of the Tribe to be de-stooled is far more terrible. Edward Heath was good enough to ask me to Macmillan's ninetieth birthday party, and produced a bottle of 1874 claret. It was still good – just imagine it was harvested when Bismark was chancellor.'

Side-stepping tricky questions like a matador, he refused to comment on the Tories' poor performance in the local elections. Didn't he think Mrs Thatcher ought to let up a little and apply the brake?

He pondered for a minute, examining his huge signet ring, once again regarding compliments to a leader he admires hugely as sucking up.

'Like her, I am a workaholic, I work fast. Some', he raised an eyebrow at two minions scribbling down every word at the end of the vast polished table, 'would say too fast. You have to look at Margaret Thatcher pre-bomb and post-bomb. She was so outstanding, showed so much courage after the Brighton bomb. She may well have suffered a little from post-bomb shock. Shock takes different forms. After I pranged my car in January, my doctor told me this. The Prime Minister carried on working without a pause. If you insist on keeping going, you may temporarily have to appear a little sterner and most forceful to stay on course.'

Having described Neil Kinnock as 'an inexperienced second rater' some months ago, he has revised his opinion.

'Neil Kinnock took that jibe of mine very well indeed, and came back with a genial and handsome answer. What he said about the Brighton bomb, his sense of outrage, was absolutely right. Basically he is a very nice man, but not I think a large figure. Denis Healey, on the other hand, is a heavyweight – a bully and a thug, but a man of great stature.'

He also has a soft spot for David Owen. 'I like the fellow, not many do. He can be brash and abrasive, rather like myself, but he had the courage to leave his *awful* party. He is a very considerable person, much larger than David Steel.'

The Alliance, he felt, had done rather less well in the local elections than expected.

'Nothing will happen until the SDP and the Liberals become one party, exchanging their twin beds for the matrimonial couch, until the blushing bride Steel says yes to bridegroom Owen, and they consummate the marriage.'

As Lord Chancellor, he is also speaker of the House of Lords, sitting on the crimson woolsack in a long wig and splendid black robes. According to Lord Longford, fellow Etonian and sparring partner over sixty years, 'Quintin's the most impressive Lord Chancellor we've ever had. He's always been frightfully theatrical of course. In fact he's far better in drag than out of it.'

While Viscount Macmillan admits the best seat in the Lords is at Hailsham's feet. 'Quintin lounges with his wig askew, and you think he's fast alseep, then he suddenly comes out with some devastating aside. He's at his best when the bishops are holding forth. Of course he knows far more about their subject than they do.'

The greatest tragedy of Lord Hailsham's life was in 1978 when his wife Mary was killed in a riding accident, aged only fifty-five. Her face, merry, lively, charming, looks out of two pale-blue photograph frames on his desk. He says he will never get over her death, and assuages his loneliness in work and by lavishing affection on little Spotty, who was now noisily crunching a Bonio on the crimson carpet. He refuses to give up his rambling house in Putney for a smaller, more central place because there'd be no room for all his books.

'He's always got a different excuse,' said a friend. 'He can be frightfully obstinate.'

According to his daughter-in-law, journalist Sarah Hogg, he is a wonderful grandfather: 'Despite his massive workload, he finds time to write to my daughter every week. The only cloud on their relationship was when she refused to be confirmed and he started bombarding her with twelve-page letters, until she decided it would be easier to give in. All his five grandchildren lecture him dreadfully, particularly on his clothes – "You can't wear that awful old shirt" – he takes it like a lamb, rather enjoys

110

it. Children adore him, because he never talks down to them.'

In the Boer War, the bullet that would have killed his father was diverted by a silver flask in his pocket. One hopes that any prospective bullet that might be given him by Mrs Thatcher is deflected by his wit and great wisdom. There's plenty of life in the old Hogg yet.

Beverly Harrell

This piece was written in June 1985, during a trip to Death Valley, while I was writing a book about Patrick Lichfield photographing nude models for the Unipart Calendar. It is interesting, bearing in mind her later fame, to note the reference to Madam Cyn at the end. Having never heard of her, I even spelt her name wrong.

Beverly Harrell is by any standards a remarkable woman. She has written a best-selling autobiography. She narrowly missed winning a place in the Nevada State Assembly. She lectures to enraptured conventions and universities all over America. But most important of all – she is the madam of the Cottontail Ranch, the most famous bordello in the Wild West.

While I was staying in Death Valley, California, recently, her Cottontail Ranch burned to the ground. Naturally it was headlines in all the papers.

Although there was a 'full house' at the time, happily all Beverly Harrell's ladies and their customers escaped unhurt except for red posteriors and extremely red faces from having to charge naked into the twilight leaving their clothes to turn to ashes. Even more heart-warming to animal lovers was the fact that all the prostitutes rushed back through the flames to rescue Miss Harrell's two poodles and a chihuahua, who were trapped in her blazing bedroom, and then risked their lives setting free the brothel's three guard dogs, whose kennel had also caught fire.

Nor was their ordeal over. When the fire engine failed to show up from Goldfield, a town fifteen miles away, the girls and their clients fought the fire themselves. According to the *Death Valley Gazette*: 'One "real" brunette was observed spraying the flames with a hose in the altogether, aided by her recent client, who was clad only in a pair of unmatched brown and black socks.'

As California is the next state to Nevada, I decided to drive over the border and visit Beverly Harrell and her brave girls. As we set out in noonday temperatures of 125 degrees in the shade, my driver pointed out a towering red rock, known as Corkscrew Peak. Appropriately, on the other side of the road, we passed a house built in 1905 entirely from 50,000 bottles consumed in one riotous night's drinking.

Brothels were legal in Nevada, my driver explained, and were to that fun-loving, hell-raising state what gourmet food was to France. One man had even produced a Michelin Guide on the subject. Having been given a massive advance by his publishers, he visited thirty-seven brothels, sampling the wares, and star-rating the girls and amenities, which included orgy rooms, jacuzzis, dominance dungeons and even nine-hole golf courses, so the wives had something to do while their husbands were inside. The author must have enjoyed the task for the book is now in its third edition.

Nevada is obviously proud of its brothels, one of the last relics of the old Wild West. Whenever there's a town celebration, the tarts, resplendent in satin leotards and fishnet stockings, have their own float.

Now the driver was pointing out a pretty ranch-style house with a very green, beautifully laid out garden, and a large airstrip. That was the Cottontail's fiercest rival, he said, Fran's Star Ranch, which sells T-shirts advertising 'Fran's Friendly Fornicating Facilities' or exhorting you to 'Have a Good Lay' or to 'Support Your Local Hooker'.

Back in 1978, Fran's Ranch suffered the same fate as the Cottontail, and burnt to the ground. All the local wives promptly got together and organised a huge street party and several charity dances to raise money for Fran to rebuild the brothel.

The landscape was getting starker, dust devils swirled, Joshua trees held up their spiky branches like praying hands. 'Business As Usual' said a large sign as we swung off the motorway up Frontage Road. At the end, surrounded by nothing but desert, creosote bushes and a few unseen

113

rattlesnakes and coyotes, we found the ruins of the old Cottontail, and Miss Beverly Harrell herself supervising the rebirth of the new one.

Bulldozers had already spread gravel over the charred ground, and three vast caravans had been towed in, so the girls could carry on working, plus a smaller caravan for Miss Harrell herself.

'This little girl doesn't sit around,' she said in the twanging voice of a Damon Runyon hood.

I was a bit apprehensive about my welcome, but Miss Harrell, a sort of Bette Upper-Midler, was affability itself. Despite orange hair not unlike that of the scarecrow in the Wizard of Oz, reddened eyes to match her square red glasses, and a pallor emphasised by no make-up, she could obviously look extremely handsome when done up.

Now resting from her labours, she was sitting in her caravan's shadow, one of the only bits of shelter from the punishingly relentless sun, reading her press cuttings on the fire. On a nearby table, a kitchen pinger ticked away to indicate when time was up for a customer.

Miss Harrell said she had been off the property when the fire started. 'I was sad when I first saw the ruins, I shed a tear, but I can't sit around and cry when eighteen years of blood, sweat and toil go up in smoke. I've got too many people depending on me. The fire started because of a gas leak in the water heater. It was a very hot night, a hot wind fanned the flames. Lee, Mona Silver, Susie, Lili and Annie were all working.'

No, I couldn't speak with any of them, she said firmly, working girls didn't like publicity; anyway they were busy at the moment. Glancing at the three caravans, I half expected to see their sides heaving.

Susie, said Miss Harrell, now gazing meditatively at the charred remains of an aspen tree and a pile of cardboard boxes, had been particularly brave, dragging out the little poodles, Frou Frou and Socks, and the Chihuahua Tinker, who had huddled terrified under the bed. From the caravan window, three furry faces yapped in agreement.

Even braver perhaps, after the guard dogs, Hooker, Rogue and Jezebel, had been set loose, and were charging panic-stricken round the desert, were the naked clients who helped

114

round them up. The dogs, being very vicious, might easily have had their hands – or something much worse – off.

'The fire engine,' said Miss Harrell scathingly, 'could easily have made it. Their excuse', which she plainly doesn't believe, 'was that two fire engines were out of order, and the only one left wasn't insured to leave the city limits. So the girls had to watch the Cottontail burn down,' Miss Harrell went on, turning round to check the pinger. 'They were very shaken, they all lost fantastic wardrobes in the fire.'

Then one girl wearing only a G-string, and another a pair of pants, and the rest nude, had piled into the car with the six dogs and driven to Tonepah, fifty miles away, where they'd stayed in a motel.

Miss Harrell refused to elucidate on how her clients got home, but said that with typical Nevadan generosity, the Tonepah locals had asked all her girls out to meals, and, when they returned to the Cottontail, had provided them with clothes, tea and, most important in this heat, ice.

'Conditions are pretty primitive at the moment,' said Miss Harrell, who is obviously a trooper with a sense of adventure. 'We're back in the old 1900 days, when the girls hauled their water, and cooked on camp fires, and the red lantern marked the tent that was being used for sex in a miner's camp.

'At least we've got a freezer and a microwave on the way,' she went on with satisfaction, and says she plans to build a bigger, ritzier Cottontail, by bringing in four massive 24 foot by 64 foot mobile homes to provide sixteen workrooms for sixteen working girls.

Although insurance will cover most of her costs, and replace the orgy room and the jacuzzi with the red lights underneath the bubbling water, what saddened Miss Harrell most was the loss in the fire of her collection of old guns, and antiques gathered over a lifetime.

'There were armoires, that's cupboards, sweetie,' she explained kindly in her Brooklyn accent, 'Tiffany lamps, Queen Anne chairs, Sheraton chairs and bordello paintings.'

She was even more upset at the loss of her library, which included works by 'Schopenhauer and Nietzsch-ee and many books on psychology', which were read more by her girls than the customers, because the television reception in the area was

115

so bad.

Her customers range from local miners to city slickers and tourists who drive down from Vegas 156 miles away. Richer clients charter planes and land on the 1,000 yard air strip. Her finest hour was when an old cargo plane had engine trouble and was forced to crash land nearby. The crew had such a good time, they stayed on at the Cottontail for nearly a week.

Next moment two extremely seedy individuals in black shades drove up saying their huge and dusty black car had overheated. Could they use the hose? One jerked his head rather unenthusiastically in my direction. Out of one eye, I could see Miss Harrell frantically shaking her head and waving her palms back and forth.

What sort of girl made the best prostitute, I asked.

It wasn't enough to have a beautiful body and face, replied Miss Harrell, beadily watching the two seedy individuals, who were now drenching the new gravel with precious water. Most beautiful girls were too imbued with their own importance, and too self-centred. A good working girl must be able to listen and be a bit of a psychologist as well.

'The customer may have had a bad day at the office,' she went on, as we both lifted our feet off the ground to avoid being flooded. 'Or had a row with his wife. He wants sexual favours, but more than that, he wants someone to talk to.'

Nevada women were enlightened, she went on, her voice taking on a singsong recording machine quality, as though she was launching into one of her lectures to universities.

'They like the idea of legal prostitution. They would rather their husband went with a working girl than partied around with his secretary, or the wife of a neighbour and broke up a marriage. Wives often drive their husbands out here. Young men of Nevada', continued Miss Harrell, ignoring the rising tide like Canute, as her voice became positively messianic, 'are far better sexually educated than in any other state. They are fortunate to have legal brothels where working girls can teach them. Men don't know unless they're instructed. Fathers bring their sons here, so they won't go into their marriages blindly.'

Anyone would have thought she was running a sixth form college.

Bordellos in Nevada, according to the guide book, range

116

from the vast five-star-rated Mustang Ranch, which has thirty-five girls working full-time, to Irish's, a brothel which, despite having the best bar in the state, with wood panelling, hanging plants and a pot-bellied stove, has the ultimate Irish joke, no girls.

The Cottontail, which also has a five-star rating, is midway in size between the two. Miss Harrell, who prides herself on quality not quantity, insists on holding classes to teach new girls how to make love properly.

'It's not fair to the girl or the man to throw an unpolished girl on the floor,' she said.

Did they practise on live men, I asked.

'I hold verbal classes,' said Miss Harrell, suddenly prim. 'I don't hold with Masters and Johnson.'

Happily married, but unwilling to discuss her private life, she believes her girls are happy working for her.

'They have chosen a profession where the remuneration is far greater than that of a secretary, a dress designer or an airline stewardess. No one is held captive here. Nor do I retire people. My oldest hooker is sixty. She's worked for me since she was sixteen.'

Any moment she'd qualify for a gold pinger.

Then, as a great honour, Miss Harrell took me over the workrooms, where I half expected to see the girls engaged in carpentry, making egg racks. Many rooms were in use, others had gold mirrors on the walls, and amber candlewick counterpanes on the beds, not unlike a Maples showroom. I had an exciting glimpse into the temporary orgy room, which had royal blue shagpile swarming over the floor and up four steps leading to the water bed, and a huge screen for porno films.

'Now you can see what a working girl looks like when she's not working,' whispered Miss Harrell, as she softly opened a door. Inside, a ravishing redhead in a purple flowered bikini was not reading Schopenhauer, but lying fast asleep on her back on the bed.

On the way out, Miss Harrell introduced me to a good-looking workman called Kent, who, grinning like a small boy in a sweet shop, was building catwalks between the caravans.

'Last night, Kent put up the vital thing to show we're back in business,' she said dramatically. 'The revolving red light.'

The pinger was pinging, the seedy individuals had turned off the hose and she was plainly restless. It was time for me to go.

'Do you know Madame Sin?' asked Miss Harrell as she walked me to the car.' 'She lives in England.'

I said I hadn't had the pleasure.

'Madame Sin gave a party for me when I was in the UK. It was full of celebrities, everyone from schoolteachers to punk rockers. A real conglamoration.'

Had she really only lost her bid for the Nevada State Assembly by 120 votes?

'I won,' said Miss Harrell bitterly. 'But they stuffed the ballot. They couldn't bear the thought of a madam in the State Assembly.'

It seems a pity we can't have a few people like Miss Harrell to ginger up the House of Commons, or at least Gloucestershire County Council.

Margaret Thatcher

This piece was written in January 1985, four months after the Brighton bomb outrage.

I last interviewed Mrs Thatcher in 1976 after she'd taken over as Opposition Leader. We spent an hour cosily chatting at her home in Flood Street, uninterrupted except by Mark and Carol drifting in and out. I was totally charmed. She was friendly, direct, touchingly insecure, and quite unlike her rather stiff, pompous, pontificating television image. She was also extremely pretty – not unlike Selena Scott's rather serious blue-stocking elder sister. The most important thing in politics, she had said, was the ability to pick oneself up, however hurt you felt inside.

She certainly needed this ability when I saw her this week.

'I'd better give you the bad news first,' she said.

With the pound crashing about her ears, I thought she was going to say she was too busy to see me. Instead she dropped the bombshell that: 'The abdominal, or abominable, or whatever they call themselves, council in Oxford have just turned me down.'

She was plainly in a state of shock. For a second, her eyes filled with tears. But predictably Maggie-nificent in a crisis, she pulled herself together, adding with a toss of her head that if Oxford was unwilling to confer an honorary doctrate on her, she had no wish to receive it.

Ironically, she was wearing an Oxford blue coat-dress and blue stockings. In her shoes I'd have rushed upstairs and flung on a Cambridge blue track suit. Despite having a frightful cold, she looked great – not a day older than when I last saw her. The turned-down air-force blue eyes are as bright as ever, the blond hair more ashy and less corn-coloured. She is also more regal and imposing.

Her study in Downing Street is more like a sitting room, decorated in gold and pistachio green with flatteringly soft lighting. A marvellous collection of pictures is only marred by a perfectly frightful seascape by Winston Churchill, which Mrs Thatcher glowingly described as 'Turneresque'.

Security was much tighter than the last time I saw her. A charming but tigerishly protective press aide asked me to submit my line of questioning in advance, and was present throughout the interview making incessant notes. She had also placed a tape-recorder between me and Mrs Thatcher so I couldn't pull a fast one. It was a far cry from the cosy twosome in Flood Street.

Mrs Thatcher clearly didn't want to talk about Oxford, so I asked her how she felt she had changed since she came to power.

'Well I don't know,' she clasped her beautiful white hands, and leant forward. 'The biggest change came with the Falklands. Somehow I never expected to be in charge of a government which had to fight a war, to deal with the military so that no one in the field was in difficulties, seeing that the military and political sides understood one another. But we found we were able to take decisions.'

'Then the Brighton bomb' – for a second, the deep contralto faltered. 'We lost very dear friends. But one found one could cope with that too. In a crisis, the way ahead is so much clearer. Then I had no idea at the start how to cope with international conferences. I went off wondering what would happen, whether there was some crucible of wisdom one could draw on. But there was no philosopher's stone. It's merely a question of being properly briefed, and doing one's homework.'

There followed more talk about coping successfully with the Common Market, as though she were comforting herself in the face of the vicious Oxford snub by recalling other times when she had displayed courage and tenacity. To cheer her up I remarked that her recent trip to China had been a success. Wasn't she pleased that the Chinese leaders, used to spitting in public, had only spat twice in her presence, compared with nineteen times in front of the Russians?

120

What was remarkable, said Mrs T, neatly sidestepping the question, was that she had seen all four Chinese leaders in one day. No other visiting foreigner had had that honour.

Didn't it help when she met leaders from abroad that she was such an attractive woman?

'I've no idea,' she replied crisply. 'I don't think they notice you're a woman, it's a question of personality and exchange of views.'

She did find it difficult however to get her point of view across through an interpreter. She was used to having one sequence of thought.

'You suddenly realise when you're well into a subject that they can't understand what you're saying, because you're speaking in a different language.'

One suspects the same thing happens in her own country. She tends to answer questions by swinging into set speeches on different subjects. By the time you've halted her, or tried to get down what she's saying in case it contains some pearl of wisdom, you've forgotten your original question.

Last time I had seen her she complained about the calibre of the Tory top brass: 'Where are my lieutenants?' How did she feel about her cabinet today?

This time Mrs Thatcher proceeded to praise her squad in Downing Street, smiling warmly at her secretary as she spoke of 'marvellously loyal support. Number Ten is more like a family than an office. A hundred people work here; it's a home and very cosy.'

I tried another tack.

Why did she personally get such a good press, and her ministers such a lousy one?

'I divide people into Doers and Communicators. We in the cabinet are doers. We get on with the job, perhaps we should spend more time communicating. I like people who talk straight, no jargon, no fudging.'

Earlier in the day, I'd seen her during Question Time being shouted down by the Opposition, who tabled a motion of no confidence in her financial policy. Watching Mrs T and Mr Kinnock bristling across the dispatch boxes, I was reminded of Dignity and Impudence: Mrs Thatcher, as the stately Great Dane, too high-minded and noble to resort to vulgar abuse,

121

with Mr Kinnock as the little terrier snapping round her ankles. Was she prepared to give a headmistress's report on Mr Kinnock's first six months leading the Opposition?

She was not – beyond murmuring that Mr Kinnock was rather discourteous, which must be the understatement of the decade. On the other hand, she added, she had also faced Wilson, Callaghan and Michael Foot as well.

How had they differed?

'I've been in science,' said Mrs Thatcher firmly. 'All my background is strategy and detail, arguing with the support of evidence to reach a conclusion.'

As her particular crosses were Mr Scargill and Mr Kinnock, I asked, did she think there was anything particularly significant about balding red-headed men?

'Has Mr Scargill got red hair?' said Mrs Thatcher, the blue eyes widening in surprise. 'Yer can't judge personality, yer know, by the colour of people's hair.'

What about beards? Did she really hate them, as had been quoted that week?

'My dear,' she threw her hands up. 'I've no idea where that came from. It has caused great upset.' Then, smiling quickly at the bearded *Mail on Sunday* photographer, who was cringing behind a saffron armchair, she added, 'I mean beards are like hair styles, they suit some people and not others.'

She would not forecast whether the miners' strike was coming to an end, nor whether Mr Scargill was going to play ball.

'What grieves us' – often she sounds like a Shakespearian king – 'is that the miners are still on strike. After ten months the striking miners have never had a chance to ballot. They must be getting terribly into debt. Why go through such deprivation,' she went on in a hurt voice, 'when they've been offered the best voluntary redundancy terms, and the latest equipment? One can't turn back the clock.'

I took a deep breath: 'People are saying after six years, your financial policy is in tatters.'

It was as though I had switched on the cold blast of my hair dryer by mistake.

'Tatters,' said Mrs Thatcher, in the outraged tones of Lady Bracknell, 'Tatters!'

Neck and face reddening like a turkeycock, she launched into

122

an impassioned party political broadcast.

'With the miners' strike into its tenth month, inflation is at its lowest for fifteen years, we are producing more than ever before; record production, record sales, record investment, the biggest denationalisation programme ever . . . 1.7 million more owner-occupiers . . . reduced taxation. Some tatters.' She sounded positively Churchillian.

The only way to tackle unemployment, she went on, was to produce more, to work harder . . . 'Spirit of enterprise . . . going out into the market . . . catching up with other nations . . . Youth Training Schemes . . . job creation programmes.'

The voice rolled on relentlessly, as though she were patiently re-dictating a botched-up letter to a junior secretary. Dazed by the torrent of words, I noticed I'd never seen better-looking potted plants. Perhaps I should start making speeches to mine about inflation and the spirit of enterprise. She was now repeating what she'd said to Alistair Burnett, the previous week, that all the socialists did was shuffle round the shekels.

She is like a wonderfully comely steamroller. One can see why most of her cabinet have the puffy look of constantly being flattened like pancakes, then blown up with bicycle pumps next morning.

'Tatters,' snorted Mrs Thatcher.

There was a long pause.

'Parkinson,' I said, desperate to raise the temperature, 'I mean Norman Parkinson, said of all the beautiful women he'd photographed, you had the most sex appeal.'

Mrs Thatcher brightened: 'How astonishing! He made it so easy. He's a professional of course. I'm a professional person. So are you. I like dealing with professionals.' She smiled suddenly – the tartar with the heart of gold, forgiving me for the 'tatters'.

One has the feeling that although she is genuinely kind and sympathetic, particularly to people in trouble, she's not remotely interested in what makes herself or anyone else tick. She never watches herself on television, for example, nor does she read hurtful things written about her in the press.

'My dear. If one is hurt, and these things do hurt, one can't concentrate on work, and nothing must interfere with that.'

Wasn't that rather wrapping herself in cotton wool?

'I read the press digest. If a complaint or criticism is justified, of course, I take it seriously. That's why I go out and about a lot. I will not be cotton-wooled. And I do put up with Question Time,' she added by way of justification.

'Twice a week,' said her press aide defensively.

'Must be a nightmare,' I said. 'Rather like doing Mother Rota at the play group.'

Mrs Thatcher laughed. 'Rather worse. Real children are far more grown-up than politicians.'

Certainly she has been dealt some terrible blows in the last few years, loosing one great friend and mentor after another: Airey Neave, Lord Carrington, Cecil Parkinson and nearly Norman Tebbitt. Lord Carrington she regards as a particularly bitter blow.

'We tried and tried to persuade him to stay. If he had been in the Commons, it would have been different. He could have come to the dispatch box and argued his case, but he was denied this. He's a wonderful man, with a great sense of people, wisdom, experience, universally respected and liked, and great fun,' she added enthusiastically, as though they'd spent rainy afternoons playing Postman's Knock together.

Would Cecil Parkinson come back?

'I don't know,' she said wistfully. 'We miss his abilities. He knew business from the inside, so few politicians do. There was no jargon, no fudging. Even rarer, he was a doer *and* a communicator.'

'He was certainly a doer,' I said without thinking, then hastily added, 'And a great communicator too.'

Despite the punishing schedule, there are no black rings under Mrs Thatcher's eyes, and hardly any lines on her face. She is alleged to work harder than any other prime minister. She attributes this to years of practice: 'I've never had more than four or five hours sleep. Anyway my life is my work. Some people work to live. I live to work.' Then, suddenly remembering the unemployed, 'That's why I feel so desperately sorry for those who have no work.'

Did she really hate holidays?

'I hate lolling about, I must do something. I can't stand sunbathing in a deckchair.'

'You could lie on the sand.'

'Never!' It was as though I'd suggested some fearful perversion.

How did she feel about being nearly sixty?

She laughed. 'Well, it seems much younger than I thought twenty years ago. It seemed ancient then. Now it seems rather young. Besides, Dennis is going to be seventy soon,' she added with a sly satisfaction that he wasn't going to be able to dodge advancing age either.

What did she miss most about being prime minister?

'Picking up my handbag and dashing down to Sainsbury's,' she added without hesitation. 'I miss window shopping too, and being able to walk up Regent Street to my dentist. We tried to go to Sainsbury's about a year ago, but we were mobbed. Such fantastic value, but of course one must make lists first, or it's dreadfully easy to overspend. One mustn't overspend.' Suddenly I had a vision that she saw Kinnock and Hattersley as naughty schoolboys rushing into Sainsbury's and loading up their steel trolleys with tuck they couldn't pay for.

She is certainly in great shape too – much slimmer than when I saw her ten years ago. Woodrow Wyatt has got her on to Vitamin C for breakfast, but she hasn't taken up jogging yet.

'Could lose a bit,' she said, squeezing a non-existent spare tyre. 'I don't like sugar, even on grapefruit, [or fudge either for that matter]. I drink black coffee. But I do like a thick sauce with fish, and fruit with meringue on top, and chocolate sauce with ice cream. I love baked potatoes too, but only with lots of butter,' she went on dreamily. But rigid self-control reasserted itself quickly.

'You just learn not to eat too much, to take the top off a tart, and scuffle around to find the fruit underneath.'

She denies she has the strongest faith of any prime minister since Lord Salisbury.

'No, no, Winston and Lord Stockton were both religious men.'

Did her religion help her when she was down?

'Yes,' she said simply.

Throughout our conversation, I felt an intruder, because I suspected the full shock of the Oxford rejection was beginning to sink in and I'd caught her at a particularly vulnerable moment. One could only admire her guts all the more. Time and again when people talk of Mrs Thatcher, they say she should follow her instincts because she is always right. She will always ask the practical question. To one minister who wanted £700 million to sort out the railways, she kept saying: 'But why do you need all that money, when there are so many porters doing nothing at Paddington Station?'

Blinkered she may be: one can only hope there's light at the end of the tunnel vision.

THREE

Hunting With The Hoorays

In my youth, hunt balls were held in vast country houses and were very, very wild. By midnight, the barrage of bread rolls was only exceeded by the squadrons of moths thundering out of the brocade as ancient four-posters heaved with occupants.

It was with excitement but some trepidation therefore that we accepted an invitation to the Cotswold Hunt Ball. Needing a dress, I borrowed my daughter's black strapless. A mild fit of sulks, because my husband said I looked like a badly wrapped Christmas cracker, gave me the excuse to sit in the back. The dress would never have got under a seat belt anyway; when my brother took his wife and daughters to a hunt ball in Shropshire, he had to borrow a horse box to accommodate the crinolines.

We kicked off with champagne at the house of the Joint Master, Tim Unwin. Those making feeble attempts to pace themselves drank Buck's Fizz. A hunting blade with a red Pentel was marking the list of forty people in the Unwin's party: 'Putting asterisks beside all the worst gropers,' he said. He had to guard his wife, he explained, pointing to an exquisite blonde. 'She's Polish, I'm Welsh. It makes for a wonderfully volatile marriage. We throw telephones at one another.'

Another beautiful blonde, Princess Michael's lady-in-waiting, floated across the room.

'I'm official lech-in-waiting tonight,' said my husband, pursuing her briskly.

The men looked even more glamorous than the women, gaudy peacocks in their different tailcoats, red with green collars for the Cotswold, red with maroon for the VWH (Vale of the White Horse), dark blue with buff for the Beaufort. Permission to wear the hunt coat – or one's button, as it is called – is given by the Master, like getting one's colours.

Soon they were capping each other's tales of earlier hunt balls: erotic scufflings in the dungeons at Berkeley Castle, Masters riding their horses round the ballroom followed by hounds. Our host remembered dancing most of one evening with a lampstand. 'Suddenly I noticed the then Master was solemnly chewing up a glass. My immediate unaltruistic thought was "Oh hell, he won't be able to take hounds out tomorrow." But he didn't come to any harm. If the glass is good, one doesn't.'

It was a bitterly cold night as we set out in convoys to the ball. Cars with silver foxes on the bonnets skidded over the roads, rattling cattle grids and lighting up the grey curls of traveller's joy and the last red beech leaves. Flakes of snow drifted down as we arrived at Cheltenham Town Hall. 'It's already fetlock deep in Stow-on-the-Wold,' bellowed a woman who had just arrived with a white windscreen.

In the Ladies, pale-shouldered women with weathered complexions fought for the mirror.

'I got bucked off into a cow-pat today,' wailed a pretty girl. 'I'll never get my breeches clean.'

'Soak them in Nappisan,' advised a large lady.

Soon four hundred people were tucking into a splendid dinner at £18.50 a head. On my left a late arrival seemed very familiar. Tall, raffish, handsome, like an unfrocked cherub making a guest appearance in *Minder*, he said he'd just left a crucial meeting in Maidenhead. He hunted with the Cotswold when business and racing allowed.

Suddenly I twigged: he was Michael Arnold, the Receiver who'd so audaciously hijacked the miners' five million pounds from a foreign bank last week.

'For what we are about to receiver,' I said, attacking my smoked mackerel.

What was extraordinary, he went on, was that he had suddenly bumped into one of the foreign bankers he'd been writing to for weeks trying to recoup the cash, out hunting.

130

Neither of them had had any idea that they were members of the same hunt.

'Gosh,' I said, having visions of wads of tenners being handed over as they whizzed over hedges.

Mr Arnold, forty-nine, started hunting only three seasons ago, but has, he said, no difficulty keeping up. 'I'm as competitive about hunting as I am about business. Nanny hunts with the Cotswold too – she picks me up if I fall off,' he added.

'My cleaner used to hunt with the Beaufort,' I said, to keep my end up.

On my right, the Master, Tim Unwin, said that one of the keenest hunts in the country was the South Wales Banwen Miners: 'We keep drafting hounds to them. They always want a hound who's a pack leader.'

Perhaps they should call it Arthur.

Discussing obsessions with hunting, Tim cited a former Master who'd left a clause in his will saying he wanted his body fed to hounds so he could enjoy one last run.

'We got round it by scattering his ashes on the hounds' porridge.'

A diversion was caused by the late arrival of three young men from the Cambridge Harriers, all with ironed hair and smooth faces, who'd gone to Gloucester Town Hall by mistake. 'Fast man across country,' said Tim approvingly as one of them sat down opposite us. He was certainly the fastest eater, and raced through three courses in as many minutes.

The band was playing 'Red Red Wine'. The brilliantly lit ballroom beckoned. Tim swept me off to dance. A wonderful dancer, his only problem was that, being Master, he knew everyone . . . and every time he raised his hand, which was firmly clasping mine, to hail some chum, I shot right out of my dress – a chintzless wonder.

As the vast floor filled with couples, red coats with flying tails clashing gloriously with the stinging fuchsia pinks and electric blues of the girls' dresses, the ballroom looked like a shaken kaleidoscope. I couldn't help feeling that as well as class hatred, an element of sexual jealousy must motivate the hunt saboteurs: people in hunting kit look so good.

131

'If we went out in rags on rough ponies we wouldn't get half the flak,' said Tim Unwin. 'People get completely the wrong idea. Hunting isn't a rich elitist sport – people of all ages and classes come out with us. We've got millers, doctors and farmers as well as knights. I always think of Chaucer's *Canterbury Tales*.'

To prove the point, at that moment our fishmonger bopped past with his comely wife, and I was able to order some cod for the weekend.

It was also nice to see the huge number of young people who'd paid £11.50 for an after-dinner ticket. Sartorially there is a complete divide between the young girls, who all wear mid-calf dresses and look as though they are going to a drinks party, and the wrinklies, whose dresses go down to the ground.

'Ever since a short-sighted brigadier mistook my varicose veins for patterned stockings I've stuck to long,' sighed one woman.

With the richness of royalty in the area, each hunt is proud of its royal patrons. Princess Anne and Captain Phillips hunt with the Beaufort, Princess Michael also. But Prince Michael remains loyal to the Cotswold. Maybe it is the secret of a happy marriage for each to hunt with different packs.

Prince Charles goes out with the VWH. 'HRH has got a triffic sense of humour,' said a VWH stalwart. 'The other day a bobbed-tail fox went past, and he turned to me and said, "Looks more like a bloody corgi." Bloody funny, what?' he brayed with laughter.

Everyone was having a great time. The Receiver turned out to be a wonderful dancer, too, what with twinkling black suede feet and long muscular arms (presumably as a result of humping all that money around).

No one poured champagne over anyone else – at £15 a bottle they couldn't afford to. And with so many starving birds outside, people were far too conservation-conscious to hurl bread rolls.

12.30 a.m.: There was a rumpus in the hall. 'No, you can't come in,' a bossy official was saying to a group of people with snow in their hair. 'The doors shut at midnight.'

The next minute a pint-sized individual in a red coat, furious as a hunt terrier, was yelling into the official's navel.

'You don't understand, you must let us in. They're hunting over me le-and tomorrow.'

Three thousand acres near Winchcombe tipped the scales, and the doors were opened.

Hungry as hunters, we fell on breakfast. Back on the floor, the fastest eater, obviously still hungry, was nibbling his partner's bare shoulder. One local Casanova, with patent leather hair and an overdeveloped little finger from winding women round it, had the unenviable problem of having both his wife and current mistress as well as his discarded mistress present. The former two smirked slightly as the ex-mistress flounced up to him, breathing fire.

To shut her up, he bore her off to dance, and all round the floor one could see them rowing in that rigid-jawed upper class way, as though they'd had too many injections at the dentist.

Why do hunting people have such a reputation for adultery? Perhaps it is because they're so fit – at three o'clock in the morning no one was flagging – or because if you like chasing foxes, you enjoy chasing other things, or because, as one man explained to me, 'Only time one can really sleep with one's wife is two weeks in November. Then she can have the baby in August, and be back in time for cubbing.'

3.45 a.m.: Sadly mindful of icy roads, we called it a day. Outside there were already three inches of snow. As the long dresses trailed over the white pavements, flurrying flakes blurred the Regency houses, and young blades engaged in a snowball fight, we seemed to have gone back a hundred years.

Not unamiably, the attendant manning the Gents sleepily imitated them: 'Going to Georgie's drinks party? Ya. Is Rose going? Ya. Hunting tomorrow? Ya. Think they'll cancel? Ya.'

Suddenly the horn called and they all swarmed back, view-hallooing, to join the stampede of the 'Posthorn Gallop'. A passionately embracing couple, nearly knocked sideways in the rush, reluctantly disengaged themselves and joined in.

The anti-fox hunting brigade don't seem to realise that by

133

trying to abolish hunting, they are taking a pair of scissors to the whole social tapestry of country life, which has lasted for generations. For, as R S Surtees commented, over a hundred years ago, the real business of a hunt ball 'is either to look out for a wife or look after a wife, or to look after somebody's else's wife'.

It has very little to do with foxes.

Arsenic For New Lace

I shall always be grateful to Shirley Conran. Halfway through last summer hols, when my children were about to murder one another, my daughter bought *Lace*. For five days total peace reigned, until she emerged from her bedroom declaring it: 'Absolutely brill, far better than *Jane Eyre*.

Unable to have a read, because another teenager whipped the book, I had to wait for *Lace Two*. Sadly it's a frightful disappointment, pretentious, pornographic, with non-existent characterisation and excruciating dialogue.

'The secret of a best-selling novel,' Shirley Conran advised me recently, 'is to write about rich, very successful people doing things the public aren't familiar with.'

Thus in *Lace Two*, we have Maxine, the French Countess, 'with only ten guests to consider, organising a simple programme: partridge shooting on the estate, riding through the vineyards, cards and conversation for those who hoped to say warm inside, and on Sunday a stag hunt on a neighbour's estate'.

During the stag hunt, the Countess, who has abandoned her sables,'so heavy and dark', for more flattering red fox, is rewarded for her sartorial discrimination by a bunk-up in a hayloft with an old admirer.

Thousands of readers perhaps do justify getting a cheap thrill from such junk on the grounds that they are acquiring knowledge at the same time. Thus as well as stag hunts, we learn about female circumcision, stocks and shares, motor racing, women's magazines, middle-eastern customs, how to decorate our houses and ourselves tastefully, and how to improve our sex lives. Superwoman rides and rides again.

135

All Miss Conran's female characters are, like herself, achievers – even the tarts. In a totally unnecessary flagellation scene, Therese is only conscious, as she whacks the hell out of an ancient client, of how much she is improving her backhand drive.

Silliness reaches pyrotechnical levels when King Abdullah, of goldfish fame in the first *Lace*, bangs Lady Swann on a billiard table in a London club during a bomb scare. Detail is so elaborate, one half expects the King to chalk the tip of his member before play commences.

Despite her regret that she is only wearing 'chainstore pantihose', Lady Swann enjoys it all enormously, telling herself: 'I am lighting up like the sun rising over the Swiss Alps, when the mountain peaks get that living pink glow that spreads slowly down the valley.' Sounds rather like German measles.

The jacket blurb tells us Miss Conran is an experienced textile designer and colour consultant. Certainly no fabric or paint shade goes unremarked on, no garment undescribed. But why doesn't she provide us with out-of-town stockists as well?

She is also heavily into fruit and food imagery, what with peach négligées, apricot sofas, cinnamon-tipped nipples, and best of all 'claret-coloured private parts'. I guess they only perform at room temperature. Perhaps I'm needled by Miss Conran's pronouncements that brass beds are *passé* (I'm very fond of ours) and, even worse, that no woman over thirty should wear grey – which means junking half my wardrobe.

Worst of all was the information that the sex goddess heroine has breasts weighing a pound each. Whimpering, I rushed to the bathroom and watched in alarm by several cats and dogs, measured my length on the carpet, and tried to weigh one of mine on the bathroom scales. Utter horrors – only two ounces. Reminding myself the bathroom scales deliberately underweigh, I tore downstairs, and tried the kitchen scales. By cheating and leaning heavily, I notched up three kilograms, but a straight single boob could only achieve four ounces. Frightfully depressing being only twenty-five per cent sex goddess.

Finally I suppose one must grudgingly admire Miss Conran for making so many millions. Perhaps, as a fellow author, I'm just suffering from Pennies Envy.

136

Dashing Away With The Smooth Iron Lady

'You've got the Iron Lady at the Winter Gardens and Rambo at the ABC – not much to choose between them,' said my taxi driver with a sniff, as he dropped me off at the 1985 Tory Party Conference. It was plain, though, as I fought my way through a forest of friskers into the conference hall, that the Iron Lady and the Tory Party were hell-bent on softening their image.

Labour's renaissance at Bournemouth had put the fear of God into them. To stop Mr Kinnock cornering the market in compassion, ministers were falling over themselves to appear the most caring.

Mrs Thatcher's hair and make-up were softer. The powder-blue platform subtly emphasised her blue eyes, which filled with tears during 'I Vow To Thee My Country'. Now she was gazing besottedly up at Transport Minister Nicholas Ridley, who was rabbiting on about buses, as though they'd just got engaged. There was Willie Whitelaw radiating paternalism, and Leon Brittan like a short-sighted camel, gazing mournfully out of its cage on the ills of the world.

Also on the platform under the sign saying 'Serving the Nation' sat my old friend and fellow panellist on 'What's My Line?', Jeffrey Archer. I resisted the temptation to wave and ask him: 'Does your party really provide a service?' Poor Jeffrey's had a bad time since he joined up, but I'm sure he'll bounce back. Maybe he should try some remedial exercises for fallen Archers.

Mr Ridley's speech finished, the main problem – as one boring cliché-ridden speech followed another and dull-egate followed dull-egate – was to keep awake. Everyone harped on the caring theme. Mrs T looked enchanted. I looked at her ministers. When I did a piece on parliament about ten years ago, I found the Tory men great fun, drinking like fishes, and exchanging sizzling eye-meets with any pretty girl that came along. Alas, Sarah Keays has had the same inhibiting effect on them as AIDs has on Hollywood. Now when they were not exuding compassion on the platform, they gazed stonily ahead, terrified of catching a lady delegate's eye, ignoring the odd bits of Central Office crumpet passing by.

There was a distinct shortage of pretty girls at the conference generally. 'All the good-looking ones have defected to the SDP,' said a photographer in disgust.

The Tory Party not only seems to have gone very down-market (the ringing voices, the hats and the pin-striped smugness have almost entirely disappeared) but also grown much older. The overwhelming impression was a hall full of favourite aunts and uncles enduring faulty microphones, forty minute queues in icy winds, because they were seriously worried about riots, unemployment, the North and the Inner Cities.

Despite these problems, and a poll saying fifty-one per cent of the electorate think Mrs T ought to be replaced before the next election, she seemed very chipper.

Speculation, however, is endless about her successor. On the one hand there are the Hair Apparents: Douglas Hurd, with his white woolly mop and pepper-grinder voice, and Geoffrey Howe of the silver curls. Sir Geoffrey's really perked up since he's become Foreign Secretary and presumably escaped abroad from Nanny Thatcher. Chief of the Hair Apparents, however, is the conference darling, the amazingly sleek Michael Heseltine. No one delivers clichés with more aplomb, but he does make the audience roar with much-needed laughter. His blond locks flopped about so much that I expected a lady delegate to rush up and lend him a Kirby grip. I suspect that, although gentlewomen prefer blonds, they tend to end up with brunettes, and both the party and Mrs T will settle for the Not-Much-Hair Apparent: Norman Tebbit.

Until he smiles, the excellent Norman looks like the second murderer in Macbeth. The perfect lugubrious stand-up comic, his forte is ripping apart the Opposition and Mrs Thatcher's enemies within the party. Once Tebbitten, twice shy. The

138

conference was enchanted to see him back on such vitriolic form after his appalling ordeal at Brighton. Mrs Thatcher awarded him even warmer glances than Mr Ridley. 'Wave Norman,' she whispered, as the delegates cheered.

I don't think Norman Fowler has leadership potential. I fell asleep during his speech. His claim, that his caring Social Services Ministry had raised single parent allowances to the highest level, didn't seem to carry much weight with Miss Keays. Ironically, her ludicrous revelations in the *Mirror* cheered up the delegates enormously. Nothing unites the Tory Party like a good bitch. It's also terrifying when one reads of Cecil's vacillations to think he might easily have been the next leader. Perhaps Miss Keays ought to adopt 'Serving the Tories' as her new motto.

While Mr Fowler banged on, yet another would-be leader, Ted Heath, sat sulking and huffed up like a great gelded tom cat whose mistress had forgotten the Whiskas.

The Wets, in fact, are so ghastly I can't see them posing any threat to Mrs T at all. Mr Pym stood sourly watching speeches from the gallery. Mr Walker of the mean collie eyes and the suspect vowel sounds keeps needling Mrs T about unemployment, but seems to care only about his own advancement. A fellow minister told me scathingly that Margaret thought by giving Peter Energy, she was sending him to Siberia. But the salt mines suddenly turned into the gold mines of the miners' strike.

On Wednesday, when Norman Tebbit made a second speech urging the conference to greater efforts to win the next election, he looked much less a leader. He fluffed several punchlines, and seemed as uncomfortable as Bernard Manning trying to play Brown Owl.

'We must play as a team,' he exhorted the delegates. 'We must revitalise every organ in the party.'

'Not Cecil's for God's sake,' muttered a delegate.

In the evening, there were plenty of parties, but they were all rather subdued. At the Institute of Directors' bash, the urbane Ronald Allison, Mrs Thatcher's speech-writer, had been given the night off because Mrs T had gone bopping with the Young Conservatives. He expected substantial rewrites on the big speech in the morning, he said. Mrs T, like all stars, got very strung up beforehand, but the more nervous she was, the better she spoke.

'I had terrible problems at Brighton last year,' he sighed. 'I'd written a viciously anti-Kinnock speech, but Kinnock was so nice and sympathetic about the bomb I had to rewrite it from start to finish, cutting out all the beastly things we'd said about him.'

On to dinner with Julian Critchley, Tory rebel, and Bill Rodgers from the SDP, who was covering the conference for the BBC. A beady Tory whip at the next table looked at us very suspiciously, speculating on what we were up to. Talk inevitably got round to Cecil Parkinson.

'The trouble with Cecil,' said Mr Critchley, 'is that he always says what you want to hear. When I was causing trouble, and he was Party Chairman, he would always put his hand on my arm, sigh deeply, and say: "What a waste." The thing I couldn't cope with was the way he was always slagging off Mrs Thatcher behind her back.'

Outside in the foyer, the hotel was offering two videos; one of *Mary Poppins*, the other of a horror film called *Christina* – 'She'll Possess You, She'll Destroy you, She's Death on Wheels,' which seems to sum up both the loyalists' and the Wets' views of Mrs Thatcher.

On balance, the people who deserved the standing ovation were the delegates, but generally I was far more impressed by Maggie's ministers than I expected to be. If they could add curing to caring, I might even vote for them.

The Teen Commandments

I was thirteen when I wrote my first book. It was called *The Teen Commandments*, and consisted of advice to parents on how to behave and not irritate their children to death. Sadly, before I could ram the book into a safe, and profit from its sage counsel in later life, I lost it.

To jog my memory, and in a faint hope of reducing the guerrilla warfare at home, I asked my own children for their list of Dos and Donts for parents.

Top of the list was unanimously: Parents should not pry.

This involved asking questions such as: 'Where are you going?' 'Who with? Will you be back for supper?' 'Who was that on the telephone?' 'Why were you so long on the telephone?' 'Was it a good party?' And (worst of all), 'Did you meet anyone nice?'

Parents should not then resort to MI5 tactics, ringing up best friend Louise's mother, asking if Louise had a nice time at the party, then casually asking if Louise mentioned Emily getting off with anyone – and then saying: 'Oh, his parents are supposed to be rather nice, aren't they?'

Parents should not force their children to go to frightful parties where they won't know anybody, on the premise that they might meet Master Right.

Parents should cook and foot the drinks bill for their children's parties, but not attend them. Nor should they invite any guest without consultation – just because a boy washes and goes to Winchester, it doesn't stop him being a wimp.

Parents should never make comparisons, saying: 'When I was your age, I had hordes of boys from Eton, Marlborough and Radley after me, but we never did anything, of course – we were so innocent in those days.'

Parents should not regurgitate the past to the accompaniment of violins, recounting how during the war they had nothing to eat, only water at meal times, and had to wash up, dry and put away because there were no dishwashers.

Parents should not automatically turn the volume knob 45 degrees to the left whenever they enter the room. They must appreciate that homework is only possible if stereo, radio and television are blaring. They must never storm into the sitting room, howling: 'I'm not having you glued to television on a lovely day,' then spend the rest of the afternoon themselves watching the rugger international.

Parents should share everything with their children: hair-driers, belts, make-up, and that utterly gross, yucky black polo-neck jersey, which was rejected with screams of mirth in the summer holidays but which has suddenly come back into fashion.

Parents should never make personal remarks. If their children wish to appear with their hair like an upside down lavatory brush, dipped in plum jam, that's their problem.

Parents should provide a twenty-four-hour taxi service and always lend their children the car to practise driving. After all, Volvos are built to withstand a few gateposts and stone walls.

Parents should not be inconsistent, howling with laughter over Adrian Mole and videos of *Animal House*, drooling over Madonna, then going berserk if their children behave in a remotely similar fashion. They should not hold forth on the perils of teenage drinking while clutching a second triple whisky. Nor is a half-empty packet of Rothmans in a trouser pocket proof of heroin addiction.

Parents should never dictate their children's diet. Four Mars bars, seventeen packets of crisps, two pounds of Granny Smiths, a litre of Coke and four mugs of hot chocolate – leaving the relevant milk-coated pans in the sink – are the ideal substitute for three meals a days.

Parents should never answer 'Yes' to the question: 'Is there anything I can do?' Nor make the most biddable child do the most housework.

Parents must appreciate that there's no time like the future. Bedrooms can be tidied next year, washing brought down next week, as long as it's then done immediately, as the child needs it before lunch.

Parents should not throw tantrums over inessentials, such as every towel in the house wet under the bed, topless ketchup bottles, encrusted forks in ancient half-filled baked beans tins behind the sofa, and twelve newly ironed shirts hopelessly creased because someone's rummaged through the hot cupboard after a pair of tights.

Children should not lose too much sleep – their mothers and fathers may just be going through a difficult, rebellious age.

But sadly, as Anthony Powell once pointed out: 'Parents are often a great disappointment to their children. They seldom fulfil the promise of their early years.'

The English Lieutenant's Woman

'I am not going to watch it on television,' said my husband, as I set out for the Abbey. 'I've got far too much work to do. Nor,' he added, eyeing my dress disapprovingly, 'should you be wearing spots, you'll just add to the wall-to-wall measles in church.'

On the way, I perked up. It was such heaven being cheered like mad as my taxi whizzed round Parliament Square, but rather disappointing that a dustcart following us was cheered even louder.

The first person I saw outside the church was Lynda Lee-Potter looking very glamorous in a sapphire blue coat and a big white hat. I said she looked very brown, she said it must be rust. We were soon joined by Jean Rook in an even bigger hat, and Peter Townend, the *Tatler* guru, who felt Fergie was 'a leetle too bumptious'.

'Bum is *the* operative word,' said a male journalist excitedly. 'She must be a tiger in the sack.'

Guests were rolling up. An enormous cheer greeted a handsome Brazilian polo player with blackcurrant ripple hair and a sinuous wife. Lady Elmshurst, the bride's grandmother, who comes into the Dummer newsagents every morning and only buys the papers with nice pictures of Fergie for her scrapbook, went by, saying what a nice young man Andrew was.

Ted Heath, more radiant than any bride because Maggie's having such a foul time, waddled past saying he was happy to talk to anyone about sanctions. Upper-class women gingerly clanked jaws to avoid knocking each other's hats off.

'I expect we'll find millions of chums once we get inside,' said

144

a beauty, looking at the press corps in dismay.

It was bitterly cold. All around me, desperate to get an angle, purple hands were scribbling purple prose. Maeve Binchey, resplendent in a tent dress and no hat, said Thank God she wasn't filing copy till tomorrow, when she could distil all the rubbish written by us hacks.

Big Ben struck ten, in we surged. The Abbey with its blue carpet, faded rose satin seats, towering nave and towering naval officers in their splendid uniforms, made the perfect theatrical set. The pulpit was topped with flowers, like a Tory lady's hat. White and pink carnations hung over the edge to catch a first glimpse of Fergie.

The press were going mad trying to identify everyone. The pillar on my left wasn't very communicative, but I had high hopes of the young man on my right who was steadily making notes. Alas, his brilliant shorthand turned out to be Arabic longhand. Beyond him a Japanese was sucking toffees.

There was much speculation as to whether a girl in tuna-fish pink in the front row was Pamela Stephenson masquerading as a plain clothes human. There seemed to be far more red-heads than usual. Mr Kinnock, for example, was looking very bullish, but so he should with such a ravishing wife in her satin coat of many colours.

As a concession to morning dress, David Steel was wearing a kilt, carefully smoothing it under him like a woman as he sat down.

There was a rumble of interest as Mrs Barrantes – a wonderfully elongated figure in egg-yolk yellow – arrived with tonsillitis and Hector. Hector, one must add, despite having forgotten to iron his face and looking like Robert Maxwell's younger brother, is jolly attractive. The second Mrs Ferguson, seated nearby, seemed far too nice to jab hatpins into either of them, but how would Major Ferguson react?

And how would Maggie react on meeting the Queen? Would they go to eleven rounds over the dwindling Commonwealth? It was all too exciting. Sitting below us now was Mrs Reagan, her huge aquamarine hat so like a swimming pool seen from the air that I was tempted to dive in and cool off.

What a pity Mr Reagan hadn't come as well, then he and the Major, who's appeared on television far more often in the last month, could have staged a Two Ronnies act.

On a nearby television monitor, the little bridesmaids and the pages, straight out of *HMS Pinafore*, were arriving at the door.

'They're so well behaved. I expect they tranked them beforehand,' said an American journalist.

People with handles to their names were now nodding to Handel's *Water Music*, and at last we could see Fergie, a radiant blur on the monitor. Her glass coach had more carriage lamps than a Weybridge Hacienda.

Then suddenly like an all-honours hand at bridge, the Royal Family arrived. There was the Queen in speedwell blue to match her eyes, which are so like Prince Andrew's; and Philip bronzed and genial, like Jason Colby without his toupée; and the Queen Mother, settling happily into her chair like a great pastel swan; and Princess Anne in A-D directory yellow, who gets prettier by the day. One forgets, too, the good looks of Mark Phillips, who, despite hardly addressing a word to his wife, chatted merrily to Princess Margaret, dashing in peacock blue. Princess Alexandra stood out in bright orange, in contrast to her husband, who keeps such a low profile that a recent photograph of them both in a Canadian newspaper described him as 'an unidentified man'!

All eyes, however, were on Fergie's friend, Princess Diana, in her Nelson hat. With her huge startled eyes, and her bare knees covered by her service sheet, and her impossibly long, beautiful legs curled under her, she looked like a colt liable to bolt out of the church at any minute.

'Isn't her outfit disappointing?' clucked a lady journalist. 'Those spots are so old hat.'

In fact she looked lovely – and if she'd worn something spectacular, everyone would have accused her of upstaging Fergie.

The excitement began to bite as Prince Andrew arrived, looking handsome, but as white as his shirt and surreptitiously wiping his sweating hands on his trousers. Prince Edward, his supporter, ghastly word, was being supportive, another ghastly word. With his boyish pink face and rather unbecoming uniform (really one shouldn't wear a brown belt with a blue suit) he looked like a trainee ambulance man.

At long last Fergie arrived, and the Little Dummer Girl soon

146

to become the English Lieutenant's Woman, set out on her long walk up the church. In her impatience to get to her prince, it was as though she were roller skating under her dress.

The Major, slightly subdued except for his punk red eyebrows, held her arm with the gentle pride of a labrador retrieving a grouse. And well he might. She looked breathtaking, her thick red-gold hair framing her face in Medusa ringlets. And the dress was a miracle – the train, glittering in the chandeliers like a huge dragon-fly wing, seemed to have a life all of its own as it rippled, irridescent, over the river of blue carpet.

Following it, Prince William, determined to give his mother a heart attack, played bumps-a-daisy with little Laura Fellowes.

'Dearly Beloved,' intoned the Dean.

Next it was Runcie. As he quavered on about the dreadful day of judgement, one couldn't help wondering how many hat pins he'd used to secure his mitre, or whether he'd had his handbag searched on the way in like the rest of us.

Everyone looked happier now. Diana, though hardly taking her eyes off Prince William, beamed several times at the bride. The Queen, whatever anyone has written to the contrary, looked cheerful throughout, far happier than she had at Anne's wedding. Maybe you relax once your first child is married. Even Philip smiled sympathetically when Fergie fluffed Andrew's names. Perhaps he won't be so shirty to Wogan about cue cards in future.

Above all, it was touching how Andrew and Sarah gazed into each other's eyes and made their vows as though they really meant them, and how after each 'I will', you could hear the great muffled roar of approval from the crowd outside. The marriage service over, one half-expected the Major to blow his whistle for the end of a chukka.

A suntanned Prince Charles, who, at last, seems to be emerging out of Princess Diana's shadow, then had to read a ludicrously convoluted lesson from 'Ephesians'. With opening sentences of 107 words, one is amazed St Paul ever got anything published.

'Lead Us Heavenly Father' was the Major's cue to step back and sit next to his ex-wife. A shade unforgiving, he never once in church or on television appeared to address a word to her. It

147

seemed impossible that two people on next door seats could sit with their thighs at an angle of 120 degrees.

In the row behind, Ronnie's son-in-law, a sturdy Australian, had been firmly placed between Hector Barrantes and the second Mrs Ferguson (if you have a supporter, why not a divider) in case, horrors, Hector tried it again.

Now they were off into the vestry. Philip guided the Queen Mother, but Mrs Barrantes was not helped by the Major, who looked as though touching the elbow she had given him thirteen years ago would have given him fifth degree burns.

So long was spent in the vestry, you'd have thought they were consummating the marriage or at least opening a bottle. Meanwhile the television cameras roamed laboriously over stained glassed windows and the more comely choir boys.

The one moment of excitement was when Mrs Thatcher, looking absolutely furious in a purple hat, chicly chosen to match the black eye she might get from the Queen, appeared on the monitor. Any minute one expected a rash of empty seats, leaving only a trail of molehills on the blue carpet. Poor Mrs Thatcher – even the unctuous Sir Alistair was beastly about her hat on television; perhaps now she's given him his knighthood, he doesn't feel the need to suck up to her any more.

Finally the organ broken into Elgar's triumphal march, and the radiant new Duchess of York, having swept a beautiful curtsey to the Queen and grinned at her mother and stepmother, set out down the aisle. But she was still Fergie, you could warm your hands on the glow of happiness, and you half-expected flowers to spring out of the molehills as she passed.

Praise should also be given to her husband, who, with his wonderfully demonstrative and un-Royal way of showing he loves her, is truly a Prince Charming. Out into the sunshine they went, and the bells and the cheers rang out, and I suddenly experienced a shaming feeling of anticlimax. Over the last few months, we've got to know Fergie so well it seemed awful not to be going along to the reception to knock back champagne and cheer her on her way.

But there was still work to be done. Jean Rook was in a tizz because her car hadn't arrived. I persuaded her to join me on the underground.

'But I haven't been on a tube for twenty years,' she

protested, looking at the gaping masses nervously. 'What does one do?'

'Put your money in this machine,' I said.

'Goodness,' said Miss Rook in delighted surprise, 'It's actually given me the right change.'

All the same, I've got a horrible feeling I put her on to a train to Putney Bridge by mistake.

Back home, I rang my husband.

'Wasn't it wonderful?' he said. 'I watched the whole thing at the Garrick with Kingsley Amis. We both cried non-stop, except when Kingsley got apopleptic about that left-footer taking one of the prayers.'

And as the golden coaches roll home, and Fergie and Andrew set off in their red helicopter, and all the royalty experts go back into mothballs until the next wedding, one Scottish genealogist got it right:

'It has been,' he said, 'a glorious glorious Sara-mony.'

Great Slugs Of Cognac

'Now we can all go and shoot red-legged partridge,' as the future Duke of Wellington sardonically remarked, when the untimely arrival of a senior officer stopped him completing his victory at Vimeiro during the Peninsular War.

Following the Duke's example and that of Shirley Conran's Countess Maxine we recently spent a day shooting red-legged partridge in Spain with the Duke of Fernan-Nunez. We stayed at the Ritz, Madrid, which is like a luxurious private house at the turn of the century: beautiful rooms, wonderful food, and a smiling maid hovering unobtrusively to pick up any clothes or names we cared to drop. There was even a 'No Molestar' sign to hang outside the door so we wouldn't be disturbed.

A pomegranate for breakfast, on the day of the shoot, with pink carnation petals floating in the finger bowls, seemed a pretty chic start, but did little to dispel my nerves. Friends who'd shot in Spain had all come back with dire stories of Spaniards being so competitive they all ended up shooting each other in the bottom.

Normally the Ritz arranges for between eight and a dozen of their guests to make up a shooting party, but today, as it was the end of the season, we were joining a private party of the Duke's friends. The only Ritz guest shooting was Richard Prior, a splendidly upright figure in lace-up dung-coloured gum boots and an inverted flower-pot hat like Pete's in *EastEnders*, who told us he was a deer consultant. Cheering him on were me, my husband, the *Mail on Sunday* photographer, who spoke fluent Spanish, and a nice, blue-eyed Dutchman from the Ritz, called Tom.

Dawn was fading flamingo pink in the east as we set off in a black Mercedes. After half an hour Tom suggested we stop for coffee. Mr Prior turned pale.

'It's very bad form to be late for a shooting party,' he said.

'In Spain,' said Tom, 'it's very bad form to be early.'

Thirty miles south of Madrid at the end of a long drive, we reached the Duke's red and white house. The Duke himself had patent leather hair, protruding blue eyes, a sad face that never moved when he talked, and feet that turned out like Charlie Chaplin's. He evidently belongs to one of the leading families in Spain, but was currently being led all over his rose beds by an enchanting yellow labrador puppy, with very black Spanish eyes.

The shoot was being run by the Duke's friend, a ravishing Spaniard called Javier Corsini, who had black curls flecked with grey, and a perfect olive tan, as though he'd been up at five and spent three hours in make-up.

'I am a professional hunter,' he purred.

'Lucky quarry,' I thought wistfully.

Mr Prior was still trying to gauge the day's form.

'As red-legs have started to mate by the end of the season,' he asked, 'if a pair come over rather than a crowd, does one leave them?'

Javier looked thunderstruck: 'No 'ere, you shoot everything.'

Nine o'clock – and the scheduled time for kick off. The next hour and a half, however, were punctuated by one Japanese car after another screeching up the drive, and another brace of gorgeous young blades, with diplomatic bags under their eyes, falling out and launching into a ten-minute orgy of handshaking and chat.

Dress was varied – like a woman's autumn fashion show at Bentalls of Kingston – and included flat caps, Tyrolean trilbys, flower pots, green knickerbockers, suede and leather trousers sawn off above the ankle, khaki cardigans and Puffas. No Barbours except ours – perhaps they only wear them in Seville.

'Aren't they faint-making?' I muttered to my husband.

'More like a lot of off-duty head-waiters,' he said sourly.

At long last we set off in Javier's Land Rover, thundering over the roughest tracks, rocks hitting our undercarriage like pop corn. Javier said he was a leetle tired, because yesterday he'd been shooting big game: 'Stag, wild boar, and follow deer' in the south of Spain with the King.

Was the King a good shot?

'The King does not like too much to shoot, he prefer the stocking.'

'Oh,' I squeaked, madly excited at the possibility of regal sexual preference.

'I too prefer the stocking,' said Javier warmly.

'Si si con suspender belts,' I said encouragingly.

'No deer stocking, you 'ave it in Scotland.'

I realised he meant stalking.

Round the corner, a crowd of beaters in sapphire blue, and a couple of policemen in black plastic hats were warming their hands on a bonfire. I didn't know whether to feel safer that in Spain it is the law to have two policemen, or members of the Civil Guard, on every shoot. Off we tramped into Clint Eastwood country – stunted trees, dusty grey scrub, soft fawn fields like the speckled breast of a thrush. All down the valley, facing a steep slope, the guns took up their positions, each with a loader and a man to pick up. We stood behind a handsome middle-aged man, who looked like Fergie's stepfather and who was wearing bizarre trousers made from green billiard-table baize – perhaps they had six pockets.

It was very quiet; all we could here was the chuckling sound of the partridge. Tom from the Ritz, who had the soul of a poet, whispered that the ground might look parched now, but in the spring I would find thousands of leetle flowers, showing off their beauty. Could I not smell great wafts of thyme?

Next minute all I could smell was gunpowder. A lone partridge flew overhead. Billiard Table Trousers potted it in one, and the poor thing cartwheeled frantically through the air, landing with a sickening thud behind us. Soon the air was full of feathers all down the line. A sparrow and a thrush were blown to smithereens. Whenever anything got through safely, I cheered and was shushed reprovingly.

Finally, toot, toot, toot, came the beaters over the hill, blowing their trumpets and squeezing the last partridge out of the scrub like tomato puree out of a tube. A long note on a hunting horn told us the drive was over.

Immediately, like greyhounds from the trap, yelling Es la

mia, the guns tore down the hill to locate their partridge, and touchingly, I thought, to put them out of their misery.

'Don't you believe it,' said the *Mail on Sunday* photographer. 'They're just hell-bent on grabbing as many as possible before the other guns get them.'

Next minute the chief beater, on a large roan horse called Robert, cantered by, with a fine hare hanging from his saddle.

'Didn't see that flap past,' said my husband. 'Perhaps the horse trod on it.'

'A hare passed me,' said Mr Prior. 'But I didn't feel I should shoot it.'

Nevertheless he had shot very well. English honour was satisfied. He was also full of praise for the shoot. The birds had come out very high, and been magnificently and carefully driven.

The partridge themselves were now laid out on the ground, chestnut and powder blue, with their speckled kerchiefs, red legs, and swollen eyes, as though they'd been crying all night at the prospect of death.

Once when I went on a shoot in Northumberland and my host encased me in green rubber from top to toe, so I would blend into the countryside, I remember asking sweatily and sulkily why the young man in the next butt was allowed to shoot in a red jersey.

'Because he's a Duke's son,' said my host. 'He can shoot anything he likes.'

Similarly the Duke's puppy was now having a field day tearing the laid-out partridges to pieces. The Duke, who wasn't shooting, watched it indulgently. The other guns less so – dying to give it a kick, but inhibited by the presence of its ducal master.

The beaters set off for the next drive barracking cheerfully, and drinking wine out of leather bottles. The police were being well primed with Ritz Cognac. It was getting colder. Javier pulled on ginger suede gloves and stylishly lent out of his Land Rover as he drove along to check the undercarriage.

The Duke, we learnt, had recently got married, at the age of fifty, and was expecting his first baby in June.

Why hadn't he married before?

'Because he had enough pipple to look after him,' said Javier, as though that explained it.

For the next drive, the guns spread out across the curve of a valley, with the two middle guns flanking a sluggish stream, fringed with rusty tamarisk trees.

'I hear a red-leg calling,' said Mr Prior poetically.

Soon, to left and right, the Spaniards were blasting away, blatantly poaching his partridge.

The third drive was distinctly hairy. We stood beside Jaime, a sweet boy, who, despite impossibly long eyelashes, was a very good shot. To our right, however, was a trigger-happy wanderer in a green Tyrolean hat called Alvaro. Accompanied by his seven-year-old son, who had the inevitable winter hacking cough, and two emaciated dogs, Alvaro was determined to shoot more than anyone else.

Thank God we had fortified ourselves with great slugs of Cognac, for the next minute, all hell broke loose. As the partridges were driven towards us, Alvaro took a pot at everything, regardless of whose bird it was.

Crash, he shattered one that came through at boot level, crash, he winged another behind him at mid-thigh.

Next minute, his gun was swinging towards Jaime.

'Duck,' I screamed.

'Where,' screamed Jaime, gazing excitedly up at the sky and nearly getting his eyelashes blown off.

I longed to hang a 'No Molestar' sign on the end of our butt. My husband and I and the *Mail on Sunday* photographer were so terrified, that, despite a ground littered with rabbit droppings and no sun anywhere, we flattened ourselves on our faces pretending to be sunbathing.

'Come and sit by me,' said Tom from the Ritz, kindly. 'Pellets seldom go through two people.'

'You'd be safer in front,' said my husband, spitting out a mouthful of thyme.

A second later we cringed as a sparrow whizzed by at bum level. Alvaro swung after it, missing it twice, then getting it with the third. Perhaps as an answer to French knickers, the Spaniards should patent Spanish knickers, khaki and bullet proof.

I was never so relieved to hear anyone as I was to hear the approaching beaters. Lobbing rocks into the stream, blowing their trumpets, and laughing maniacally: 'Ha, ha, ha!' they sounded like a cross between Louis Armstrong, and Mr Rochester's mad wife.

At the end of the drive, Alvaro went bananas, scuttling round, gathering up every living thing he could find, urging on his rangy dogs. Having shot fourteen partridge, he was distraught only to trace thirteen. Unseen, his pointer, who had blond ears and a snub nose like Jill Bennett, was so hungry it had gobbled up a partridge whole.

Once again the bag was laid out, and the Duke's puppy, his mouth full of feathers, played Don't Pass the Partridge.

Back for lunch, past stunted vines, spreading for miles over the dull brown earth, like some German war cemetery. A partridge pecked at the side of the road.

'Push off,' we hissed, 'Alvaro's behind us.'

Inside the Duke's house, the walls were covered with tusks and antlers, and paintings of the Duke's big-nosed ancestors putting ringed white hands on the heads of small proud dogs. Above the Duke's coat of arms crouched a predatory looking bat. We all tried to translate the Latin motto. 'Your blood is my tea,' was the best suggestion.

The Ritz had provided a sumptuous lunch of consommé, square inches of Spanish omelette, ham, smoked filet mignon and strawberry shortcake.

Alvaro, with a glass of Rioca in his hand instead of a 12 bore, turned out to be gentle and charming. He worked in the Ministry of Commerce, he said. His dogs were called Sago and Cash Payment. Being one of seven brothers had made him very competitive. He had shot since he was seven. We were joined by Jaime of the long eyelashes, who said he worked for American Express. If my husband hadn't been present, I might have been tempted to say, 'You will do nicely, sir.'

The Duke of the sorrowful contenance held out his glass for more red wine, and said about eight shooting parties a year were held at his house, but he seldom shot himself, being a very bad shot: 'I couldn't even 'it the sun.'

The house had been requisitioned by the Russians during the Spanish Civil War, he went on. As an act of spite they had burnt it down when they left, so it had to be completely rebuilt. There was no sign of the Duke's new wife, nor, although the guns

155

nearly all wore wedding rings, of any other wives or girlfriends. Perhaps, as the Ritz had provided lunch, there was no need of them.

After lunch the sun came out, like a make-up artist gilding the rushes, adding blusher to the tawny earth and painting deep blue shadows in the grooves of the hills. We could smell great wafts of thyme now. For the last drive, which is invariably the most do-or-die of the day, we stood at the bottom of another steep hill.

'Good infantry country,' said my husband approvingly. 'The Duke of Wellington always preferred to accept the enemy whilst occupying the reverse slope.'

All along the line with no thought that the din might put off the birds, the guns laughed and chatted. All except Alvaro, who was shifting tigrishly from foot to foot, hands clenched on his gun, like Virginia Wade about to take service.

Pow, he brought down a partridge, then another, followed by a couple of lapwing, a seagull, two sparrows and a starling.

Suddenly we were amazed to see fearless Tom, darting through the firing lines as though he was at Vietnam, with an outside mandarin in each hand like grenades, bearing sustenance to Jaime and Javier. Next minute he was scuttling back to take Cognac to the Civil Guard, who sat under an olive tree, getting more civil by the minute.

To the extreme right of the line, the admirably ethical Mr Prior shot fewer than the others, because he still wouldn't poach, or wing the beaters' standard bearer, who, despite Javier's howls to keep out of sight, insisted on standing on the brow of the hill waving a fertiliser bag on the end of a stick.

'Under normal circumstances,' said my husband disapprovingly, 'he'd have been picked off by our side, since he's giving away our position.'

'You can waste a lot of cartridges on liver spots and bumble bees in the afternoon,' quoted Mr Prior philosophically, as the last trumpet sounded.

'Well shot, Richard,' yelled Javier.

'Well restrained, Richard,' chorused his English fans.

'The best shot of the day', my husband could be heard telling the *Mail on Sunday* photographer, 'was when Alan Lamb got that four off his leg which won us the game in Sydney.'

156

Camouflaged against the green, the guns came up the valley. The 188 partridges and sundry other birds that had been shot, were laid out in pairs, like some ghastly danse macabre. They looked so pathetically small and few compared with the humans who proudly surrounded them.

Then as a perfect *coup de théâtre*, a Ritz waiter solemnly approached with glasses of Cognac for everyone on a silver tray. As a royal guest told the manager of the Ritz, Madrid, recently: 'There are only two hotels in the world: this and Claridges.

Apart from the slaughter, it had been a splendid day out. But as we sped north in our black Mercedes, the Western sky was flecked with rose-pink bars. I hoped it was a sign that the 188 red legs were winging into heaven.

Ping Pong In Wiltshire

Part One

In the beginning was the talking snake, who was probably an opinion pollster in disguise. Everywhere Eve went, he slithered after her, clipboard tightly coiled in his tail, pestering her with questions about her love life: 'How many time-s-s-s do you have s-s-s-ex a week? Do you always achieve s-s-s-atisfaction?'

Eventually, Eve got so fed up, she persuaded Adam, with some help from God, to move to a less salubrious area outside Eden.

I'm not fond of opinion polls either. I find it hard to believe them (well would you tell the truth about your sex life to a total stranger?), they make me slightly uneasy about my life, and they are always contradicting each other. Just before Christmas, for example, I read that MORI had decided that the national average for having sex had risen to three times a week. It used to be 2.4 and one had been smugly aware of being well above the norm. Immediately I started worrying about how I was going to fit in an extra .6 during the Christmas rush, and with the exhausting palaver of getting the children back to school I might even slip – horrors – below the national average.

Then earlier this month a survey in a popular Sunday informed me I was in the group least likely to have an affair, because, as the mother of teenagers, I'd want to set them a good example. Reading further down the page, I was surprised to find the contradictory information that, as a woman of forty-eight, I was in the age group most likely to have an affair, because it was my last chance of a fling.

I was just contemplating jumping on the milkman when in

158

The Times last week, a sex therapist called Dagmar O'Connor told us that the message from America is loud and clear. Affairs are *passé*. Monogamy is back in fashion. They're all so panic-stricken about sexually transmitted diseases, you can't pass a street corner in New York without some soothsayer warning you to beware the march of AIDS.

According to an American friend, you have to produce a medical certificate before anyone will sleep with you. And as the easiest way not to catch AIDS is to stick to the same partner, getting it right sexually with them has become of vital importance.

Dagmar O'Connor has therefore written a new book called *How to Make Love to the Same Person for the Rest of Your Life and Still Love It*. And Miss O'Connor, looking like a strict but kindly headmistress, certainly has some whacky ideas for gingering up our sex lives. She begins brightly with the belief that few of us are abnormal sexually, but that most couples suffer from unequal desires. She goes on to quote one husband and wife whose sex life had reached an impasse because the man wanted it every day and the wife was refusing to sleep with him.

Miss O'Connor suggested that from now on the husband could have as much sex as he wanted, but whenever he asked for it his wife had to take the initiative. For the first week he went berserk, like a small boy in a sweet shop, wanting it the whole time. By the second week it was down to every other day, and by the third and fourth weeks he was happy to have it twice a week, which was quite OK by her. He had only wanted sex all the time when it seemed he couldn't have it at all. He assumed, because his wife had rejected him, that she no longer loved him.

I have always believed, like trying to re-heat cold baked potatoes, that once passion is dead you can't revive it. Miss O'Connor disagrees and recommends titillation. One exercise she suggests is taking it in turns to touch each other all over except for the sexual organs. The person doing the kneading has to carry on for forty minutes, rather like making bread. Then you change roles, or rolls, and you become the dough, shutting your eyes and letting your fantasies wander. You are not allowed to cheat and have sex at the end. But evidently, after a few sessions, couples leap on each other like rabbits.

The most common cause of lack of desire, it seems, is hidden

159

anger. A wife who won't sleep with her husband is often secretly fed up with being stuck at home with the children and too much housework. Equally, if the husband has too demanding a job, or is bossed around too much, then he will cop out as well.

One of Miss O'Connor's most bizarre solutions, if a couple are so burning with mutual resentment they can't make love, is, instead of sex, for them each to take a string bag full of ping-pong balls and have a duel in the nude at about ten yards.

One couple who tried it came in next week, smirking. They had cheated and made love, they cheerfully admitted. It wouldn't work in our house. We've got only one dented ping-pong ball, and that belongs to the new kitten. And at 90p for a half-dozen, new ping-pong balls are far too expensive anyway. Finally, my husband got stuffy and refused to have a go because he said it would bring the game into disrepute.

Another of Miss O'Connor's theories is that people's sex lives improve when they're feeling slightly naughty. One quaint suggestion was that the wife should put her foot in her husband's crotch at dinner parties and wriggle it around. That wouldn't work in Gloucestershire, where the husband would naturally assume it was one of the house labradors.

Other ideas (like ping-pong balls) seem rather pricey. You fork out for a baby-sitter, then spend the night in a motel. 'We signed in as George and Martha Washington,' giggled one couple. 'The clerk smiled, we felt really naughty.' That stickler for truth, George Washington, must have turned in his grave.

The author also has a bee in her bonnet about sex being more thrilling when one was a teenager, and believes we should re-create teenage skills: long, smooching kisses, petting sessions for hours in the back row. The latter should appeal to rugger players.

An even wilder concept is that we should regress to teenage giddiness and rediscover the lost art of mentally undressing people: 'Imagine their bosoms, bellies, buttocks, and their sexual organs.'

I did try. Setting out for the village the other morning, I passed two ancient, woolly-hatted men from Stroud District Council in orange trousers, looking into a trench. I was so busy imagining their bellies and bosoms (something wrong there), and myself as the trench, that I bumped into a telegraph pole and stubbed my chilblains.

Next I met our neighbour's eighty-year-old gardener, and tried to visualise his long white body, but got distracted when he insisted on talking about frost pockets. Then the vicar passed on his bike, and, as it's nearly Lent, I looked the other way.

Finally, the junior dog, who has no such inhibitions, took off after her boyfriend, the milkman's dog, and I gave up.

Even more outrageously, Miss O'Connor suggests you should install a full-length mirror in the bedroom, then strip off and make a speech to your partner, describing the beauties of your private parts. Then he makes a speech describing his. I wonder if one is allowed an autocue.

The next step, it seems, is to play doctors and nurses, in bed, which appears to turn on couples no end. One woman got so excited she festooned her husband's organ with pink ribbons like a barrister's brief, another started singing to her husband's member – 'Willy nae come back again', presumably.

All this makes me feel that the Americans are very, very different from us, more enthusiastic, earnest, naive and far, far less self-conscious to be receptive to these kind of ludicrous games. But I agree with Miss O'Connor on one thing: that people – particularly women – don't set enough time aside for sex. We think nothing of spending hours a day cooking our husbands' dinner, working, polishing, walking dogs, visiting friends, watching television, gossiping to our children. Sex so often seems to be last in our priorities, and if you leave it to chance it doesn't happen.

Often, it's a real effort when one's tired and preoccupied to psych oneself into a receptive mood. But, as one man said: 'It's like jumping into the pool. Once I'm in, I adore it.'

Many, however, may balk at Ms O'Connor's idea of ringing every Wednesday night on the calendar to be set aside for four hours of love. No television is allowed, which is tragic, as I'd miss *Lytton's Diary*. The telephone is taken off the hook. Then she suggests, you simply take two tuna fish sandwiches and a bottle of wine to bed and fool around.

My husband was appalled. He said he'd need at least a crate of wine and the corkscrew would be the only thing that did any screwing, because he couldn't stand all those sandwich crumbs in the bed.

161

According to Ms O'Connor, however, couples who tried the experiment found they were leaping on each other again and again. If it catches on here, it's bound to send the national average rocketing up (not to mention sales of tuna fish and ping-pong balls). So we can all start worrying all over again that we're not having enough sex, and graduate to tinned salmon and shot puts.

Part Two

I was touched and heartened recently by a story a man friend told me about a beautiful but tremendously respectable sixty-three-year-old woman. Blushing furiously, she suddenly informed him, she's had to give up the chairmanship of the local W.I. because now her husband had retired, he liked her home in the afternoons, so he could make love to her. How marvellous that he feels like that after forty-two years of marriage.

But can a marriage survive that long without a good sex life? In the past, it had to, because divorce was so frowned on, and society required couples to stay together. I suspect sex in those days was something couples often enjoyed, but didn't worry about too much.

Today, alas, so much emphasis has been put on sexual gratification, that if our sex lives aren't absolutely perfect we worry ourselves into a frazzle. One girl friend, for example, absolutely exhausts herself looking after three young children, working a full day in the office and cooking her husband a proper dinner before sleeping with him every night. Having removed him from his first wife, because she offered a more adventurous sex life, she's now terrified of losing him if she slackens off. Conversely another girlfriend boasts that she only sleeps with her husband once a year on his birthday. He is demented with misery, but puts up with it because he loves her so much.

Marriage often survives today because one of the partners is having a good sex life with someone else. Instead of working to improve their sex lives, couples start looking around. A local Don Juan excused his constant infidelities recently by claiming that his wife didn't mind because, when he had something good going on the side, he was so much nicer to her. 'And she also cleans up on guilt presents,' he added smugly.

162

Equally I was staggered at a very large dinner party in Wiltshire the other day, when the hostess gave a new meaning to the word intercourse by literally disappearing in the middle of dinner (between pudding and cheese to be exact) with one the male guests. No one batted an eyelid with they returned twenty minutes later. Meanwhile the poor husband was left gritting his teeth, not least at having to keep the priceless sweet white orbiting *and* orbiting the table.

People I find will endure infidelity and not being slept with, if they're not humiliated too much. For the sake of her children, one girl friend endured both for twenty years. Then her husband took his latest bit of fluff to stay in their house in Spain – the house that the husband had built and the wife lovingly decorated for their retirement, where all the locals liked them and assumed they were happily married. Suddenly something snapped, and she walked out.

If you are frightened of loneliness, wrote Chekhov, do not marry. Certainly nothing is more lowering night after night than the broad turned-away male back of a man who doesn't want to sleep with you. But it doesn't necessarily mean he's found someone else. He may just be frantically worried about some problem at work. Nor do marriages necessarily survive because a couple appear to be having riproaring sex.

'Nancy was sleeping with me twice a day, seven days a week, right up to the day she shoved off,' announced one outraged husband just before Christmas.

One would have hoped with all this attention to sex that people's sex lives might have improved dramatically, but sadly this doesn't seem to be the case. When Ann Landers, a hugely popular American columnist, asked her women readers whether they would prefer to be held close and talked to tenderly, and forget about the act, an incredible ninety thousand women wrote in – nine times that of a normal opinion poll. Seventy-two per cent said their sex life was so ghastly, they would willingly give it up for good for the sake of the odd cuddle and a few kind words from their husbands. And before you dismiss this as American hysteria or say that only women with lousy sex lives wrote in, our own *Woman* magazine's findings, based on a long and reasoned questionnaire filled in by fifteen thousand readers last year, came to the same dismal conclusion.

163

Nearly two-thirds of them were miserably unhappy with their sex lives. They were fed up with mechanical grabbers who jumped on them without any subtlety.

Another chilling finding which perhaps explained why so many women are prepared to go without the act was that only forty-two per cent of wives and twenty-four per cent of unmarried women ever achieved orgasm through straight intercourse. But so conditioned are women by the belief that straight intercourse is the only adult way of achieving orgasm, if they don't succeed they think they've failed. Even worse, so that men shouldn't think they've failed, two out of every five women fake orgasms. This means bleakly that forty per cent of the wives who've been moaning in apparent ecstasy in their husbands' arms all their married lives are actually pretending. It's called 'the act' because you need to be a good actress.

The main problem seems to be that, unlike their American counterparts, who are only too ready to tell a man what they want, and often frighten him off in the process, English women find it incredibly difficult to talk about their sexual needs. Half the women who had awful sex lives held back from asking for something that would have given them more pleasure because they were embarrassed. Most unspoken requests were for oral sex, manual stimulation and more affection and cuddling.

Many of them felt men want sex too much. Since I heard that one man insisted on making love to his wife, who had agonising cancer, up to the day she died, I am prepared to believe any crassness of some men. On the other hand, I do think, as a sex, they've been having a difficult time. At the beginning of the sexual revolution, we women were so busy flexing our pelvic and abdominal and vaginal muscles during intercourse, as we'd been told by *Cosmopolitan* and the sex manuals, that instead of achieving any pleasure, our heads nearly fell off.

In the same way men have been conditioned, certainly those over thirty, to believe that the great lover plunges his elbows into ice buckets and distracts himself by memorising Latin verse and the county cricket teams of his youth, and keeps going all night, in order to satisfy a woman. And often he does magnificently. But with a large number of women, he is having to suddenly learn additional skills, like having to switch to a manual gear box, after a lifetime of driving automatics.

164

No wonder men have started faking too. As one man told a sex therapist recently, 'There reaches a point when I'm tired, and I want it all to be over. With my faking, I get out of it quickly without the woman feeling bad.'

What then is the answer out of this dismal impasse? For both partners to buy a lie detector? I've never thought there was much harm in faking occasionally when you're tired, but not all the time. Nor will anything be achieved by confessing after ten years that all the moaning and the ecstasy were only a sham. Why not have two large vodka and tonics, and suggest something else as an extra, saying: 'I've read that it's marvellous, why don't we give it a whirl?'

A wife too should try to be both more selfish and unselfish in bed, not only lying back and not feeling guilty about letting her husband do the things she loves long enough to give her pleasure, but also giving pleasure in return when it's her turn.

A good sex life also needs imagination and novelty, whether it's a change of location, dressing up, reading pornography or watching blue movies. Although I do wish they'd have better actors in the latter. Peggy Ashcroft and John Gielgud would be much more convincing than all those frightful models.

Sex also needs privacy. It is surprising how few couples have locks on the bedroom door. And if you can keep the lines of communication open, it's amazing how sex lives can pick up after the children leave home or go to boarding school, or university, and the husband and wife have more time for each other.

Marriages are also more exciting if there's some sexual tension. My grandmother once told my mother that she'd rather enjoy it if my grandfather fell for another woman, as it'd be such fun luring him back. In one of the best sexual liaisons I know, on top of the bedroom wardrobe for twenty years ready packed have been two suitcases. As a reminder that at any moment either partner could walk out. They never have. But if you're not entirely sure of someone, you make more effort to please them.

Pleasing people, on the other hand, can be a problem. A girl friend rang up her husband at his office just round the corner, and begged him to rush home because she had an exciting sexual surprise. Five minutes later, there was a vigorous tantivy

165

on the doorbell, and as he was always losing his keys, she tore downstairs and opened the door wearing nothing but a heavy chain belt to find the Mayor of Reading in full regalia paying one of his random visits to see what his people thought about their rate increases.

Finally, a French princess once wrote that the perfect marriage is a hearth and a horizon. She meant that a couple should not only warm and comfort and cherish each other but also have something to strive for together, whether it's decorating a new house, advancing their mutual careers, bringing up children and, perhaps most important of all, ever improving their sex lives. For good sex is the language of love, it binds people together, it is gloriously pleasurable. It is also the best sleeping pill and sedative in the world.

Excuse Me, Your Slips Are Showing

Two ravishing young girls came to cricket last Sunday. It was their first visit, they said. As their carefully ironed cotton dresses flapped frantically against their blue frozen legs, and through the blizzard the white distant figures of their boyfriends might easily have been mistaken for polar bears, they looked utterly bewildered.

Now that spring finally appears to have arrived, many more girls all over the country will be experiencing their first cricket match. As a grizzled campaigner of twenty-four summers, I feel I should give them a few tips.

For a start, as a cricket groupie, you abandon all lie-ins. Most cricket matches are at least fifty miles from home and go on all day, so it's up earlier than the lark.

Secondly, one's clothes are always wrong. If it's tropical when you leave home, it's bound to be arctic or pouring when you arrive. The only answer is layers: a Barbour, over a Puffa, over a Guernsey, over a shirt, over thermal underwear, so you can peel off. Don't forget the shirt. Zero temperatures at home, by the law of sod, mean heatwaves at the ground, and you'll be microwaved in a cashmere jersey.

Not that it matters what you look like, since you abandon all sex appeal the moment you reach the ground. There is something about donning virgin white and playing cricket that temporarily de-sexes the male. Cricket, remember, is the only sport – like a strip in reverse – where the crowd clap a player for putting his jersey *on*.

Rather like prep school boys who insist that their mother comes to speech day and then ignore her, a cricketer feels it's wet to be seen talking to his girl friend, and it's not cricket to

167

chat up anyone else's.

Thus an average day will go rather like this. You arrive at the ground to find that the opposition, which is probably called something daft like the Fleet Street Fairies or the Bisley Buffaloes, is as usual five men short. Joyfully your beloved will scuttle on to the field to make up the numbers. When the rest of the Fairies eventually show up, he'll promptly put on a white coat.

This, alas, is not the cue for you to indulge your handsome-vet-and-comely-pet-owner fantasies, he is merely off to umpire. Umpiring will be followed by a stint in the scorebox, only interrupted when he has to bat at number eleven. Whereupon he takes a spirited swipe and is clean bowled. He then spends the rest of the match fielding.

If a very good looking player gives you a hot, come-hither smile, run like hell. He is not after your body. He is a weekend father, or a father who's only been allowed out if he takes the children. He will have three little monsters in the boot and will want you to look after them all day. Ditto if he wants you to look after his dogs – unless they're large and furry, and can double up as a rug.

Take loads to eat. Some clubs only provide lunch and tea for players, and there is a feeling anyway that because the chaps have been indulging in manly exercise, women ought to hold back. Being outside all day, albeit doing nothing, makes you wildly hungry. Cricket in fact is the antithesis of those fasting, resting Sundays so beloved by women's magazines, when you lie in bed sipping lemon juice with sliced turnip on your face. Last week, I ate six ham sandwiches, three egg sandwiches, half a Battenburg cake and four scotch eggs, to mop up the alcohol which was keeping out the cold – which leads me on to:

Take loads to drink. Many pavilions don't admit women, and most only provide beer. Last Sunday I got through one bottle of vodka, one of whisky, four bottles of Muscadet and six cans of lager, admittedly aided by two dozen other spectators similarly suffering from hypothermia.

Your survival kit should also include a Jeffrey Archer, or at least two Dick Francis (you have twelve hours to kill), all the Sunday papers (at least players wanting to read them will be forced to come and talk to you) and green foundation to tone

168

down your purple wind-fretted face.

When your boyfriend is batting, you *must* watch the game. If you find it confusing, remember batsmen tend to run after they've hit the ball. If they hit it a long way, for some reason they don't. If it strikes you on the ankle it's a four, on the head it's a six.

Do not clap and jump up and down noisily when someone drops a catch, even if it's clouted by your beloved: it's considered unsporting. Do not flash. It's tempting to keep looking in the mirror to check how ghastly you look, but it may flash sun in the batsman's eyes.

Do not talk as the bowler is coming up to bowl. If you get really lonely, get up and walk in front of one of those big white screens, just as the bowler is running away from you. Everyone in the ground will then shout and wave at you.

Never go to the loo: something exciting like a wicket falling or your boyfriend hitting a six always happens. However he gets out, say: 'That was an *absolutely* brilliant ball. Even Botham wouldn't have got near it.'

When he's bowling or fielding, put on dark glasses, so he won't know if you're watching, and get stuck into J.Archer. Then just before close of play, nip round to the scorer, and find out who your beloved has caught and bowled and congratulate accordingly.

Keep a fiver for after the game. He'll be provided with beer from a bottomless, endlessly circulating jug, and will be so engrossed in his own innings, he'll forget about your drink. If you find yourself stuck for conversation with one of the players, merely ask: 'What do you think about Boycott?' The ensuing eulogy/apoplexy will last at least fifteen minutes.

Never offer to do the teas. It's very hard work, and you always get the quantities wrong and are forced to divide a Bakewell tart between thousands, or to eat fish paste for the rest of your life.

Never offer to wash cricket sweaters, they always shrink or run. Never marry the club secretary. Your spare time will be spent typing out fixtures or team lists. One girlfriend said it was only after four years, she realised A.N.Other wasn't a player.

Never marry the captain either, or your night's sleep will be punctuated by players crying off tomorrow's game on the

169

excuse that they've 'suddenly been laid low – retch – by the most awful – retch – shellfish'. After they've finished retching they put down the telephone and say cheerfully to their wives: 'That's OK darling, we can lunch with Fiona after all.'

Unless you are truly hooked avoid Test Matches; they go on too long. I've never forgotten hearing a young man at Lords saying heartily to his shell-shocked fiancée. 'Don't worry Lavinia you'll get the hang of it by the fifth day.'

Having said all that, I must concede that cricketers away from the ground are the nicest men in the world. For cricket as a game requires unselfishness, imagination, patience, honour, perseverance, the ability to withstand boredom and to smile at misfortune, never letting it throw you off balance. All crucial qualities in a husband.

And there are blissful moments – in 1961 at Headingley when two mongrels ran on to the field with a banana skin and held up play for two minutes. In 1964, when my husband made a hundred against the Bank of England after a morning wedding reception. In 1976, when there were endless heat waves, and finally in 1982, at a charity match in Somerset, when an inebriated middle-aged streaker rushed on to the field, and Lesley Crowther who was fielding was heard to remark: 'I couldn't see what she was wearing, but it certainly needed ironing.'

Please Keep To The Footpath

From the top road, the village of Bisley, with its church spire and ancient blond houses, nestles in a cleavage of green hills like an insurance poster promising a serene and happy retirement.

The promise is not an illusion. After twenty-five years in London, we moved here four years ago. There have been no regrets, probably because we were incredibly lucky. Some villages are unfriendly and soulless, others hopelessly intrusive. But we have stumbled on a magic one, where the old are cherished, the widowed or divorced comforted, and the newcomer welcomed. When we arrived, a local hostess even gave a big party to introduce us to everyone.

There is such a strong community spirit, however, that they do prefer new arrivals to settle here, and contribute something to the life of the village. During our first year, I had frightful flak which totally mystified me. Every time I walked up the High Street, someone would come up to me and sourly accuse us of planning to move on.

This, I eventually discovered, was because everyone in the doctor's waiting room was flicking through the tattered copy of last year's *Country Life* which had originally offered our house for sale. Not checking the date, they automatically assumed it was on the market again.

The acid test, however, was whether we were going to live here, or just use the house as a weekend retreat. Weekenders who strut around in ginger tweeds, force up the prices of cottages beyond the purse of young local couples, and don't use the local shops, are not popular. There was great glee last winter in a nearby village, because some arriving weekenders turned their car over a few miles outside. No one was hurt but their

Jaguar was irredeemably impregnated with imported curry destined for Saturday's dinner party.

Not that anyone needs to import anything here. Besides a marvellous hairdresser, an excellent garden centre and a superb restaurant in the High Street, there is an amazingly sophisticated village shop which sells everything from videos to vine leaves, and attracts custom from miles around.

And there's so much to read in their windows: 'My pet chicken is missing,' says a current notice. 'He is four, and has vanished from my garden. He is very frenndly and is cawled Mary.' [sic] And you only have to pop inside the shop to find out anything – whether your daily or your secretary or even your husband is about to leave you. The gossip is so good, in fact, that a local peer implored the owners to install a chaise-longue so he could lie listening all day.

Most villages thrive on gossip, but are outwardly unfazed by it. No one betrayed any excitement four years ago, when a handsome Marquess and his beautiful wife moved into the big house, but when the leaves came off the trees, it was noticed how many of the locals had taken up bird-watching.

Equally in my brother's village in Northamptonshire, there was wild excitement when a member of Shawaddywaddy moved in and, even better, decided to get married in the village church. On the day, the police put yellow cones along the High Street and gathered in force to hold back the crowds. My brother, intent on weeding the herbaceous border, got very tightlipped when my sister-in-law, my two nieces and my mother, aged eighty, all clambered up a ladder on to the flat roof of the garage and settled down with deck-chairs and several bottles for an afternoon's viewing. To their disappointment, only six guests and no rock stars showed up.

Back here in our village, they've recently introduced a Neighbourhood Watch Scheme, which gives everyone a splendid excuse to snoop legitimately. Jeff, our Saturday gardener, who, in between bursts of frenzied weeding, sleeps in his car in the drive, was outraged recently to be roused from deep post-elevenses kip by the police who'd been alerted that a suspicious-looking character was parked near the Coopers' house casing the joint.

But if you're not into snooping, there's still masses to do here:

172

skittle evenings, pony club discos, clay shoots, men-only chocolate cake competitions at the local fête, lectures on glass blowing at the W.I. and wonderful tobogganing and skiing in the winter.

Indeed it's a good idea to wait a few months before joining anything when you arrive at a village. A bookseller friend who retired to nearby Oxfordshire, and was worried he might be bored, got himself on to every village committee in the first six months, and spent the next ten years extracting himself.

Although my husband has joined the British Legion and the Cricket Club, which slightly makes up for my non-participation, I still feel guilty that I don't have time to run up a sponge for the Distressed Gentlefolk. Recently I went along to their Nearly New Sale, and found the usual lack of charity which surrounds charity events prevailing:

'Look, look at that lovely bargain I got for 50p,' said a fat woman brandishing a tweed skirt.

'You'll never get into that,' said her friend, crushingly. 'That was mine.'

Living here in Bisley in fact is rather like being in an overseas posting in the army. Not only do most of us wear the khaki uniform of Barbours and green gum boots, but just as you can't afford to have a screaming match with the Major's wife over the bridge table, as you'll meet her at the Colonel's drinks party that evening, in a village you can't sack or fight with someone, as you'll find yourself stuck beside them in the hairdresser's next morning.

Nor can you bellow at some dog walker for trespassing on your land, because ten to one, you'll have to eat humble pie because your *own* dog has used their guinea pig as a cocktail snack. A friend nearby, whose Jack Russell ambitiously seduced a prize winning Airedale, tried to placate the enraged owner by offering to whizz the Airedale down to the vet and pay for an injection to abort the puppies, only to be told that the Airedale's owner was Roman Catholic and passionately disapproved of abortion. The row continues.

People in the country have a slightly different attitude to animals. If a pheasant waddles across the road, they are not above urging you to accelerate; and their dogs tend to sleep outside, and, bored and cold, start wandering round the village.

173

One, howling recently in the High Street at midnight, was pelted with pickled onions by the woman living opposite. Unfortunately, the following day, an old lady slipped on one and broke her leg.

Village life is happier too if, again like the army, you stick to a few rules. Keep to the footpaths; look after the badgers; don't cut down trees unless they're dead and you intend to plant some more; pay all local bills on the nail; say 'please' and 'thank you' in the village shop or you won't get bread saved for you when the village gets snowed up. Don't hide your notice applying for planning permission under the honeysuckle, so no one sees it, then put up some hideous modern house in the middle of the village.

Attempts to preserve the unspoilt quality of any village, however, can land one in trouble. Recently, an absentee landowner applied for planning permission to build a house and two garages on his field next to us. Egged on by some locals, I wrote a powerful letter to the council, larded with purple phrases about the rape of the Cotswolds, and how the hearts of generations of wayfarers had been gladdened by an unimpeded view of the village, which roughly translated meant I didn't want a lot of yobboes throwing crisp packets on to our land.

Planning permission was duly refused. Imagine my horror, at a dinner party a week later, when I discovered the handsome, but rather bootfaced man on my right was the returned and very present landowner.

Most villages are resistant to change. Our village idiot, much beloved, remains the village idiot and not a seriously disadvantaged rural person. Gays of both sexes are regarded with suspicion.

'I wouldn't go near 'er, Jilly, she's basstard quee-eer with another woman.'

And because the Cotswold lanes tend to be full of black labradors rather then black people, when a policeman from a nearby village took up with a glorious coloured girl, there was much huffing and puffing. Finally a local worthy headed the protest saying he had nothing against those kind of people, but why couldn't she go back to where she'd come from.

'Come off it,' said the policeman in amusement. 'She was born in Stroud.'

174

Similarly when our revered landlord retired after twenty-five years from the Stirrup Cup (known locally as the Stomach Pump) the new landlord got the job principally because he was the one applicant who said he didn't intend to change anything until he sussed out what people really wanted.

The Stirrup in fact is a mini Citizens' Advice Bureau. Here you can learn how to increase your marrows, decrease your docks, and dispatch your wasp plague. My husband endeared himself to the clientèle early on by trying to grow the first U-turn carrots in a seed box.

Here you will meet the great local legends, the doctor, so loved that a road was named after him when he retired, a farmer who was so good at imitating the cuckoo that he had local Colonels writing to *The Times* every January, and Leo Davies, a huge bear of a sheepdog, known as the Dogfather, who has sired most of the puppies in Bisley, and always howls at the church bells.

Here too the Cotswold Hunt meet, once a year. Four stalwarts have to block the doorway to stop the gaunt, greedy hounds charging the bar counter and wolfing all the plum cake and sausage rolls, and everyone catches up on hunt scandal: how a handsome husband has changed packs from the Beaufort to the Cotswold to ride beside his new, much married mistress; how the village lecher has been banned from the Hunt cocktail party for lurking in some comely lady rider's garden at dusk.

But if gossip circulates at Bisley so do presents. Open your front door on a Saturday morning, and often, covered in dead leaves, blown in by the bitter winds, you'll find pots of chutney, half a dozen Japanese anenomes, or a newly shot pheasant or even a hare. A copse of poplar saplings given us by our next door neighbour when we first arrived is now over twelve feet tall.

Soon after the trees arrived a local builder rolled up with a dustbin in which swam a huge golden fish, poached from a nearby Abbey for our pond.

'It's an orfe,' he said. 'We called it Eff.'

Some villagers are more reluctant to receive. An old lady refused some sticks of rhubarb recently because she hadn't got a dish long enough to cook them in.

But there's always something to laugh at here. Currently the

175

great excitement is that Philip Howard (of Graduate Gardeners), the local landscape gardener, has moved into a new house, where he's building a splendid U-turn drive with an underground car port, flanked by a huge wall, known locally as Howard's Way.

'How high is the wall going to go?' I asked my very good friend, the milkman.

'High as possible,' he grinned. 'His mother-in-law's moving in opposite.'

But the laughter is always gentle. Pretension is chiefly what makes people chunter in a village, like the male half of a couple (who work for a weekending video millionaire) referring to himself as an estate manager, when there's less than two acres to manage; or like a local snob (nicknamed Tugboat because he chugs from peer to peer) who, on being asked the other day if he had any ducks, replied: 'Only on the upper lake.'

In other villages people take fearful revenge. One Wiltshire landowner hated his neighbour so much that on learning his neighbour's daughter was getting married and holding the reception in the garden, he deliberately moved three hundred pigs into the next field on the wedding day. Another villager in Hampshire, who'd been ordered not to take a short cut across her neighbour's field, organised a sponsored walk along his footpath of two hundred dogs who hadn't been let out all day.

In Bisley, to warn neighbour not to fall out with neighbour, there is a tiny lock-up, built in 1824. Here, too, Nemesis proceeds at a more leisurely pace. The ex-landlord of the Stirrup, who was also the village undertaker for some time, was ruminating the other evening about a local schoolmistress who'd bullied them all unmercifully when they were little boys.

'I got my revenge in the end,' he added with quiet satisfaction. 'It was me that laid her out and buried her.'